CRM in Action

CRM in Action

Maximizing Value Through Market Segmentation, Product Differentiation, & Customer Retention

Dr. Ken K. Wong

U21Global Graduate School | University of Toronto

iUniverse, Inc.
Bloomington

CRM in Action:
Maximizing Value Through Market Segmentation,
Product Differentiation, & Customer Retention
Copyright © 2011 by Ken K. Wong

iUniverse books may be ordered through booksellers or by contacting:

iUniverse
1663 Liberty Drive
Bloomington, IN 47403
www.iuniverse.com
1-800-Authors (1-800-288-4677)

ISBN: 978-1-4502-7988-8 (pbk)
ISBN: 978-1-4502-7989-5 (ebk)

Printed in the United States of America

iUniverse rev. date: 1/21/11

To my wife Winnie, and my family members Hello Ma, Hello Dad, and Hello Chiu

Thank you for your love, understanding, patience, and confidence.

About the Author

Dr. Ken Kwong-Kay Wong

Dr. Ken K. Wong is a U21Global Marketing Professor and Subject Area Coordinator, training corporate executives and MBA students from over 70 countries. In 2008 and 2009, he received the Faculty Excellence Award, and was honoured in all three award categories, including: Outstanding Professor, Most Innovative Professor and Excellence in Online Education. Since 2003, Dr. Wong has been developing and lecturing marketing courses at the University of Toronto's School of Continuing Studies and also at various institutions of higher education in North America.

Dr. Wong's research interests include marketing for luxury brands, customer relationship management, and online education. His articles have appeared in peer-reviewed international journals such as *Telecommunications Policy*, *Service Industries Journal*, and *Journal of Database Marketing and Customer Strategy Management*. Dr. Wong is also the author of the SCS lecture series in the areas of International Marketing, Advertising, PR & Publicity, E-Business, and Retail Merchandising. His latest work includes *Avoiding Plagiarism, Approved*

Marketing Plans for New Products and Services, Putting a Stake in the Ground, More Bucks Annually, and *Discovering Marketing in 38 Hours.*

Prior to entering the academic field, Dr. Wong was the Vice President of Marketing at TeraGo Networks (TSX: TGO) and had previously served as Director of eProduct Marketing at the e-commerce division of PSINet (NASDAQ: PSIX). He had also carried progressive product marketing roles at Sprint Canada and TELUS Mobility.

Certified by the American Marketing Association as a Professional Certified Marketer, Dr. Wong completed his Bachelor of Science degree at the University of Toronto and holds the International MBA degree from Nyenrode Business Universiteit in the Netherlands. He earned his Doctor of Business Administration degree from the University of Newcastle, Australia and has completed executive education programmes at both Kellogg and Queen's.

Table of Contents

Foreword

Today, we are living in a period of chaotic transition - defined by the instantaneous flow of information, "all-the-time" communication, extreme competition, pervasive business complexity and rampant globalization. The pace of change has become so rapid that companies need to rethink their approaches to Customer Relationship Management (CRM). As we move towards advanced customer analytics, sophisticated customer-facing technologies are the new battleground. Now customers have more choices than ever before and insist on the flexibility to conduct business anytime, anywhere and through any device or media.

To meet heightened customer expectations, companies must now shift their business focus from the efficiencies of supply chain management to the effectiveness of demand chain management by directing their efforts toward identifying, acquiring and retaining profitable customers. CRM now in its third stage of evolution, the most exciting time in its history. From the early days of contact management, CRM has evolved into "Social Customer Relationship Management" (SCRM). SCRM is catalyzed by social technologies and utilizes the power of the cloud – in short, CRM is becoming multi-directional. Facebook, Twitter, and other social media platforms have made the fabric of the Internet richer. At long last, it's all about customers and their needs - their dialogue and relationships can finally become the true focus of CRM. It's no longer about technologies - the future of CRM will be social, transparent and customer-centric.

Social media is pushing customer relationships to a new frontier; creating risks and opportunities, exposing strengths and weaknesses, rants and raves, almost anything, that anyone, from anywhere, wants to say about your brand. Suddenly, what used to be private conversations between you and your customers is now public. Social CRM strategy is about customer engagement, not customer management. There is a fundamental shift in the dynamic between a company and its customers. Customers see themselves as part of a community that engages in shaping the company's behavior and the brand's values.

This book has been written to help readers think about the multiple facets of customer relationship management – from strategic imperatives to tactical implementations. It will help you think about how well you integrate your customer relationship management applications, program design and business processes with the rest of your marketing and customer service strategy. The advancement in social technologies will only accelerate in the coming years. The SCRM of tomorrow will differ significantly from the SCRM of today as disruptive technologies continue to emerge. The one thing that will not change is the need to focus on the customer, engaging, crafting and enhancing their experience.

My hope is that you will find this book very practical and will be able to refer back to the book as a resource when you eventually apply your ideas at work.

Idris Mootee
CEO of Idea Couture
Author, *High Intensity Marketing*

Preface

Customer Relationship Management (CRM) is one of the key modules in my marketing course. Virtually all of my MBA students have heard about this term and many of them can proudly name the top CRM software vendors in the market, but very few students can practically tell me what CRM means from an organizational perspective. Although all my students agree that CRM is important to an organization's success, most of them unfortunately have no idea where or how to start the initiative.

The lack of fundamental concepts of CRM has prevented many of these students from making the best use of their CRM systems that cost them thousands if not millions of dollars. Some students even enter the endless cycle to change CRM vendor every few years when the expected return on investment (ROI) is not achieved, without realizing that the underlying problem is actually a business and not a technology one. If you do not know about your customers or understand why they select your brand, it will not help too much even if you have got the most expensive CRM package from the best vendor on this planet.

When I sit down with my class to discuss these CRM challenges, our conversation often leads to a thorough discussion of market segmentation, product differentiation and customer retention strategies. I find that mastering these academic theories and concepts well is a prerequisite to getting the most out of any CRM implementation, no matter which software vendor has been chosen. As such, I am writing this little book to help you better understand your customers, with the ultimate intention to increase your organization's competitive advantage through launching suitable products/services that fit with their needs.

Although many of my students have reviewed the materials presented in this book, I know it is not perfect; in fact, it is far from perfect. As a writer, I would like to receive your feedback on my little book. Your suggestions greatly help shape the future edition of this book; so please do not hesitate to drop me an e-mail.

Dr. Ken K. Wong   黃廣基 博士

Ottawa, Ontario, Canada
Nov 5, 2010

e-mail: ken.wong@utoronto.ca
e-mail: kwong@u21global.edu.sg
Twitter: http://twitter.com/drkenkwong
Web: http://www.introductiontomarketing.ca/

Acknowledgement

In completing my book, I have drawn support from many people and thus feel a huge debt of gratitude. I would like to thank the International Editorial Board for providing me with valuable input and constructive criticism to my work.

International Editorial Board:

Abdalla Gholoum
Annie Nyet Ngo Chan
Basil Pathrose
Chee Wai Hoo
Dutta Bholanath
Ekaterina Leonova
Engelbert Atangana
LH Kho
Khurshid Jussawalla
Kishore Pai
Lothar R. Pehl
Narendra Nesarikar
Rajen Kumar Shah
Richard Anthony
Shama Dewji
Tasneem Tailor
Vicky Yan Xu
Vien Cortes
Zulfikar Jiffry

PART 1　CRM: An Introduction

Chapter 1—Introduction

What This Book is All About

Instead of telling what this book is about, perhaps I can try explaining it the other way around:

1. This book is not a buyer's guide for Customer Relationship Management (CRM) software.
2. This book is not a user guide for your CRM software.
3. This book will not teach you how to write programming scripts for data analysis.

Having said that, this book will stimulate your intellectual curiosity in CRM and is a step-by-step guide to analyze your customers, products, and organization. The ultimate outcome is to help extract meaningful revenue from your customer base even as keeping them happy.

In this book, I will introduce some key academic concepts such as demassification, segmentation, product differentiation, branding, and positioning. As my students would agree, the best way to master a subject is to learn through examples; so plenty of interesting examples are presented in this book. As this book is written for people who are new to marketing, I am not going to confuse you with highly technical terminology and formulas. If you are a marketing expert, this book will help refresh your knowledge about CRM and perhaps learn something new at the end.

The 4 Key Stages of CRM

So what exactly is CRM anyway? If marketing is all about the Marketing Mix (4Ps), then CRM is all about the following 4 major activities:

1. Customer Value Segmentation and Selection
2. Customer Attraction
3. Customer Retention
4. Customer Expansion

The fact is that an organization serves customers who come from all walks of life. Is it in the best interest for the organization to serve all of these customers and treat them equally? I do not think so. Hence, the first step in CRM is to divide the customer base into different segments, understand their different needs, and then select the most profitable (or having the highest growth potential) customer segments to focus your marketing efforts. The second major activity in CRM is customer attraction. To get potential customers excited about your product or service, you need to walk the extra mile in product design. The third stage in CRM is customer retention. After all, your business will not be sustainable if you suffer from a high customer churn rate. The last step of CRM involves getting existing customers to spend more with your organization.

In my opinion, CRM is not simply a software application or system for tracking client data and activities. It is a strategic business tool that can be used effectively for business growth. With a solid understanding of the CRM concepts, an organization's proprietary customer data can be leveraged to find new prospects, cross-selling opportunities, and potential conflicts of interest among channels or departments. In the ideal world, CRM should serve as the single point of contact to help understand customers' needs, and apply knowledge from previous interactions with customers to design better products, services, and business processes for your target customer segments.

How This Book is Organized

This book has 10 chapters and they are being divided into 4 major parts. In Part 1, I will introduce you to the concept of adaptive enterprise and show you how customers' explicit and implicit needs can be identified. In Part 2, the segmentation basics will be presented. The fundamentals of market segmentation are introduced in Chapter 3 and common ways to segment the consumer market are shown in Chapter 4.

For senior managers who are already familiar with the basics, they will appreciate Part 3 as it touches upon advanced segmentation strategies for the consumer market. The 8 Mental Models are explored in Chapter 5 while the P-Types and VALS-Types are examined in Chapter 6. Subsequently, strategies for business market segmentation are discussed in Chapter 7.

Once the various segmentation strategies have been discussed, we will enter the final part of this book to talk about creating customer stickiness. I will introduce you to the concept of product differentiation in Chapter 8 and show how companies are able to create competitive advantage by designing superior products and services that stand out from the crowd. As learned from the marketing or economic classes, consumers are often irrational when it comes to shopping time. Hence, the key concepts of branding and positioning will be revisited within the context of CRM in Chapter 9.

The final stages of CRM include customer retention and expansion. Some winning formulas to retain valuable customers will be presented in Chapter 10. Concepts such as switching barrier, churn management, and customer life-time value analysis will be explored. Up-selling is an interesting topic on which a few pages are dedicated as well.

A side-effect (or side-benefit?) of reading this book is that you may be able to save some money in your day-to-day life. This is because some marketing tactics that companies use to attract, retain, and upsell customers are presented. Having a good understanding of their tactics may help you select the financially-optimal product or service that can save some good money in the long run. Are you ready to begin this exciting learning journey? Let's begin!

Chapter 2—Do you know your customers' need?

What is an Adaptive Enterprise?

The very basic concept of CRM is to sell your customers the appropriate product or service that they want, at a price point that they are willing to pay. In the past, a good coffee shop was a place where coffee beans were ground on site and good coffee was being served. But today, tell me what do people do at Starbucks or Second Cup? If my guess is correct, people surf the net, do homework, listen to music, or just hang out there with friends chatting. Of course, the coffee has to taste good or else nobody will go there, but the key success factors are no longer just superior coffee beans. In today's competitive market, the key success factors (KSFs) of a good coffee shop include complimentary Wi-Fi Internet, nice jazz music, romantic ambiance for socializing, and sufficient power-plugs around the shop to ensure patron's laptops can be charged, even if they are working on their laptops for hours.

In 1992, Stephan Haeckel first introduced the term "Adaptive Enterprise" and concepts such as "Sense and Respond" and these concepts became popular with his book titled "Adaptive Enterprise: Creating and Leading Sense-And-Respond Organizations" (published by HBS Press in 1999). His idea is that an organization should aim to be "adaptive" so that it can "sense" customers' need and "respond" with the right offerings. A company that only focuses on "make and sell" without realizing the rapid market change is vulnerable.

To give you an example, consider the computer floppy disks. If you are old enough like me who came from the Apple II and IBM 286/386/486 era, you might still remember those lovely 5 1/4" and 3 1/2" floppy disks of the old days. Virtually all top manufacturers of floppy disks went bankrupt in the 1990s when CD-ROM became the industry standard for file exchange. How about those top manufacturers of CD-ROMs? Many of them went out of business subsequently because they did not realize that in the 2000s, people are using USB-sticks that are more portable, durable, and hold much more data. How about those top USB-stick manufacturers? Some of them are currently struggling because people in 2010 are storing and exchanging their files directly onto the Internet "Cloud" over social networking platforms such as Facebook. The world keeps changing; so where will these top social networking providers be in 10 years time? If they do not adapt themselves and remain too satisfied with what they have today, you can easily guess their fate when history repeats itself.

Become an Adaptive Enterprise

Being an adaptive enterprise involves two fundamental business actions: Sense and Respond. In reality, many organizations fall short in these areas because they are focusing on "Make and Sell"; they are not willing to get out of their "comfort zone" to make changes in the way they do business. You may have heard about these lines often in the office:

"If it's not broken, don't fix it!"

(Ken: But there may be better ways to do things faster, cheaper, and more efficiently!)

"We've been doing this for years so keep doing it."

(Ken: Even the best product or best business strategy won't last forever. Just like the stocks, past performance won't guarantee future success.)

"I don't think our customers are complaining…"

(Ken: Are you sure? Don't tell me that you're referring to your empty "comment box" located in the reception area, or that seemingly working e-mail box called complaints@yourorganization.com. People these days are talking about your organization in their blogs, online forums, Facebook, and Twitter pages!)

"We'll never be able to match our competitor because we have limited resources."

(Ken: Why not? Remember that you only need to be great in key features that your customers care the most! There's no need to spend your budget too thin. Got a shoestring ad budget? Then just choose the right channel to advertise.)

"It's risky to be an innovator, let's be a fast follower instead."

(Ken: Sure you can be a fast follower. However, if you don't run fast enough, you will easily fall behind other fast followers in the market as well. Your No. 2 market position may easily become No. 8 or 9 in just a few years' time.)

"We are No. 1 in market share."

(Ken: RIM has the No. 1 market share in the smartphone market, but how come people are lining up on the street to get their Apple iPhone 4 but not RIM's Blackberry Torch 9800? Having a large market share has little business value, unless you're working in the aircraft manufacturing industry where the product life cycle is really long.)

As you can imagine, the word "Change" can be a scary one and you will certainly hear all kinds of reasons why maintaining "Status Quo" can be good. But history has already shown that evolution is unavoidable and one must adapt itself to the new market environment. After all, the only constant is change. The following pages show the steps for making good changes in an organization.

Sense Your Customers' Latent Needs

Aim to fully understand your customers' problems, including the expressed and latent needs.

If your significant one is telling you, "Honey, I need some Yoga pants.", can you identify the expressed and latent needs from this statement? The expressed need is obviously the acquisition of a pair of Yoga pants, but the latent needs include many things, such as a need to (i) get better health, (ii) increase self-confidence, and (iii) meet people who share similar views of life.
A walk into a Lululemon store shows that it not only sells a wide range of Yoga garments and accessories, but also organizes all kinds of free Yoga sessions and events to bring Yoga practitioners together. Lululemon's shops are always staffed with Yoga professionals with whom you can meaningfully discuss anything about Yoga. Perhaps the most interesting observation is that Lululemon displays its garments on plastic figures that come in different heights, sizes and shapes. This makes people feel better because not everybody has a tall and slim body type like those fashion models in Paris. With this understanding, one can see why people are willing to pay a premium price for their Yoga goods at Lululemon stores.

Respond with the Right Solution

Try to address customer's needs by developing "solutions" and not just "products" or "services". These solutions have to be much better than your competitor's by several orders of magnitudes.

Let us say you are one of the national telecommunication incumbents like Bell or TELUS. If a business customer comes to you to buy a "T1 line" for Internet connection, do you just sell them a "T1 line" and that's it? Of course not! What you need to do is to step back and think what your customer is really trying to accomplish. Business customers do not buy a T1 line to watch Youtube or play Facebook in the office. Perhaps they are hosting some mission-critical applications in house. If that is the case, a complete solution would include not just the T1 line, but also some load balancing routers to ensure high server availability. By having a thorough understanding of your customer's need, you may even be able to sell this business customer some value-added services such as network monitoring, remote data backup, and security/IT auditing. By providing your customer a complete solution that addresses its business needs in a one-stop shop manner, you increase the "stickiness" that helps to reduce churn down the road.

On the consumer side, a visit to this toyshop called "Build-a-Bear Workshop" is an eye-opener. Is it just selling stuffed animal toys? No, this shop is actually providing the kids and their parents the "opportunity" to work on some small projects together. It is the toy-making experience, and not the toy itself that the parents are paying for. Now one can understand why the shop is packed even when a typical stuffed animal costs $30+.

Respond Through the Right Channel

Consider how people learn about the latest fashion trends. In the past, fashion designers mainly advertised their products via direct mail pieces, magazine ads, and window displays at the retail level. But now, advertisers are spending money on e-mails marketing, blogs, and social networking platforms. The upscale fashion brand CHANEL has even developed an iPhone application to put exclusive product offerings at customer's fingertips. Internet has changed the way people conduct business and it is not surprising to know that since Christmas 2009, Amazon has been selling more e-books than hardcover books.

Dell used to sell computers directly via their own web site and call centre, but now you can find their kiosks in shopping malls. Even some low-end models of Dell are now available in mass retailers such as Wal-Mart. So why is Dell practicing "channel reintermediation"? I think Dell is trying to target different market segments that it might not be able to access otherwise from its existing direct web and phone sales channels.

As you can see, the way companies advertise and sell their products keeps evolving. If you think you have got the best channel strategy today, that is good, but planning for the future should not stop. Consumer behavior will change and this important fact simply cannot be ignored.

Respond with the Right Message

Some companies just "blast" their promotional e-mails out to the world with a dirty or outdated mailing list, without realizing that their e-mails are reaching existing customers as well. Even if you are targeting existing customers for upselling, do you know well in advance the kind of service or product that they are currently buying from your company? Marketing dollars need not be wasted by asking customers to buy something they have already been using.

In the ideal world, you should know a little bit more about your customers, for example, their age, nationality, preferred communication language, and residing location. Equipped with such information, promotional messages can be customized thus obtaining the required effect. Instead of asking a 75-year-old customer to log into their online account to redeem an offer, how about asking him or her to visit a local authorized dealer to talk to somebody? There are still people who are not Internet savvy and this customer segment cannot be ignored.

Respond at the Right Time

When was the last time you talked to your customers? Before they make the purchase? During the purchasing process? Two months after they have made the purchase? Or do you only talk to them when they express their intention to churn? Instead of sending your churned customers tons of "switch back" offers in a passive manner, a proactive role to offer some incentives to your customers for renewal two or three months before their contracts end would be a better method.

Some companies fall into the trap of providing 24/7 support because they want to provide immediate response to a customers' enquiry. However, the fact is that a company's subject matter experts (SMEs) will mostly go home at 6 pm and will not stay overnight, therefore there is no higher-level support to the front line staff at night, especially if the night shift has been outsourced to call centres overseas. Having front line people without proper support at night can be harmful. Complaints such as "The online chat agent is an idiot, he has no clue what I'm talking about!" and "It's a waste of time! I was on hold for 15 minutes but the call centre rep just couldn't solve my problem and asked me to call again tomorrow morning!" are not uncommon.

The solution? It is better not to provide 24/7 support unless the right people are in place to handle these calls and online enquiries. In general, customers are reasonable as they also work from 9 am to 5 pm in their own companies. Manage customers' expectation and do not frustrate them with over-promised customer service.

Respond Respectfully

If some customers do not want to receive e-mail marketing messages, allow them to have their names removed from the mailing list easily. It does more harm than good if customers are bombarded with unwanted e-mail or direct mail pieces. Even if customers have opted to receive your messages, do not abuse them by sending out e-mails every week. It is called Spamming. In 2010, the UK marketing team of Ben and Jerry's Ice-cream decided to shift from the use of e-mails to social networking sites to communicate product offerings to their customers. The reason? E-mail marketing campaigns are costly and the ROI was dropping fast.

Means-End Chain

Marketers often make use of a framework to analyze consumer's need to come with up the right marketing message and product offerings. It is called the "Means-End Chain" analysis. In simple terms, this analysis asks to identify the attributes of a product or service (the "means"), explore their consequences, and reveal the personal value that it brings to the consumer (the preferred "end-states") as reinforced by the consequences.

The core idea is that consumer's decision making is all about evaluating and choosing alternative actions to reach the desired end-state, and not necessarily about selecting a product. When the product's features can be translated into values that consumers care the most, this product will be chosen.

Let us illustrate the use of Means-End Chain with an example in the banking sector. When most of the Canadian banks are having similar financial products and rates, why would one choose a particular bank over another? In Canada, most banks operate from 9 am to 5 pm but do you know that most TD Canada Trust branches are open from 8 am in the morning till 8 pm at night? This bank is well known for its long branch hours. In the United States,

TD Bank even opens on Sundays! Using the Means-End Chain, let us identify its Attribute, Consequences, and Values from the above-mentioned example:

Attributes (i.e. What are the qualities that make the product function in the desired manner?):

Long Branch Hours

Consequences (i.e. What will the product do for the consumer? What benefit does it provide?):

As a customer, I do not have to rush to the bank during lunch time or after work

Values (i.e. Why are these consequences important to the consumer?):

1. More Family Time – I can go home earlier after work. Being able to look after my kids earlier is priceless.

2. Better Health -- I do not have to skip lunch anymore just because I have to do banking at lunch hour. Having a proper lunch is important to me because I have stomach ache.

So, what does this analysis mean to a marketer at TD Canada Trust? Perhaps the benefit of having more family time when people use your bank can be advertised. By understanding the "values" that consumers are looking for from your product or service, a better marketing mix can be formulated to cater to their needs. At least, it provides another angle to look at your unique selling propositions.

Consumer Behaviour — The 5-Stage Buying Process

In the study of consumer behavior, one of the most important concepts is the "5-stage buying process" that explain people's decision-making process in purchasing.

The 5 steps are:
1. Recognize the problem
2. Search for information about the issue

3. Evaluate possible choices
4. Decide about purchase
5. Evaluate purchase

To illustrate the process, let me use a simple "umbrella purchasing" example that I personally encountered recently. I was writing this book at a nearby Starbucks but as I left the coffee shop, it started to rain heavily. I had to leave because I promised to see my wife in another location in 30 minutes. Unfortunately, I did not carry an umbrella with me and I also did not drive that day, so my problem was "I'm going to get wet with this rain" (Step 1).

Some people surrounding me were waiting for the rain to stop but I could not wait forever; so I pulled out my smartphone to check the weather forecast (Step 2). Well, the web site said that the rain would continue throughout the day and the severe weather condition warning was issued for my city. Sitting at the coffee shop to wait for the rain to stop was not a smart choice. So, what could I do next? (Step 3)

It seems I had several options at that moment. I could run across the street to buy an umbrella at the Rexall pharmacy to save myself from the rain, or just run in the rain bravely. The latter option was not a good one as I might damage my laptop and get sick as well. So, walking across the street to Rexall was my only feasible option. The smart folks at Rexall put a rack of umbrella and also raincoats at its store entrance. Should I get an umbrella or a raincoat, I wondered? (Step 4).

The raincoat was cheaper but Rexall did not have my size, so better buy the umbrella. Would I get into trouble by buying this overpriced black-color umbrella? Mind you I have got a few of these at home already. But because I had the cash to spare and I absolutely could not be late that day to meet my wife, I believed the purchase of an umbrella was a good choice (Step 5).

As you can see from this example, a consumer like Dr. Wong will buy an ugly-looking, overpriced umbrella when it is able to help him solve the problem. If not for that crazy rain, he would never buy such an ugly-looking umbrella!

So, what is the learning here for marketers? Find out what kind of problem your product or service can solve for your customers, and particularly under what kind of situations. Then, adjust your marketing mix accordingly to maximize sales opportunity. In this example of the umbrella, the manufacturer has to ensure the pharmacy stocks up these products sufficiently during the heavy rain season, and that the low-end, inexpensive models should be sold at these store locations for quick sales. If the umbrella were $100, I would rather walk in the rain!

A Few Words about Problem Recognition

When you analyze your customers' problem, try not to look at the obvious ones. Using banking as example once again, the problem that bothers people may not be the low interest rate in the savings account or the limited variety of investment tools that your bank provides. Try to put yourself into their shoes and you may realize some other kinds of challenges. For example, you may be dissatisfied with your current bank because…

1. The banker does not speak my mother-tongue language
2. The banker lacks expertise in my industry and it is like talking foreign languages with him or her when discussing my business financing needs
3. The bank's operating hours is too short! How come it is always closed whenever I need to visit the branch?
4. The bank does not have global representation outside of North America
5. The banker does not seem to respect me because I am not a millionaire

See, people's dissatisfaction toward your organization may not be directly related to the product or service, but related to "how" they are treated or served. By having a good understanding of your customer's concerns, these problems can be corrected earlier to keep the customers happy.

PART 2 Segmentation Basics

Chapter 3—Dividing Your Customers into Groups

What is Market Segmentation?

Market segmentation is the process of splitting customers, or potential customers, within a market into different groups within which customers have the same or similar requirements satisfied by a distinct marketing mix (4Ps). In simple terms, customers often have different needs and wants so you divide them into groups to better serve them. In general, marketing segmentation should be used at any time you suspect there are significant, measureable differences in your market. However, you may be wondering why this exercise of breaking up your customer base into different groups is an important one? In my opinion, there are five good reasons to do that.

1. Demassification: The Mass Market Has Disappeared

Still remember how you bought coffee in the 1980s at a local coffee shop? The choice was simple at that time; the choice was between a regular coffee or decaf followed by the cup size, and that's it. If one wanted something more sophisticated, a cup of cappuccino or espresso could be ordered. There was no need to think too much when ordering because most coffee shops served coffee virtually the same way, as if everybody had the same needs. The way to achieve business success in the old days focused on a few concepts, such as centralization (to control quality), standardization (to ensure the same user experience), mass marketing (advertise to everybody), and mass production (to drive down the production cost). Even if companies were willing to adapt, incremental adjustment could be realized with no major changes.

As you might have noticed already, the business world has moved away from treating everybody in a similar manner to making customers feel personal, as if everybody has his or her own needs. A visit to a nearby Starbucks may drive home the point when one can hear somebody ordering something like…"Can I get a Tall extra hot soy with extra foam, split shot with a half squirt of sugar-free vanilla and a half squirt of sugar-free cinnamon, a half packet of sweetener, and put that in a Grande cup and fill up the "room" with extra whipped cream with chocolate sauce drizzled on top?"

This might be a little bit exaggerated but the fact is that the barista is willing to customize your coffee order to make you happy. In fact, many coffee chains are turning this customization ability into their competitive advantage to better differentiate themselves from others.

As futurist Alvin Toffler once predicted in his best seller "The Third Wave", the products and services that we buy will get more personalized, customized and demassified. The "One-size-fits-all" approach to do business is gone. Take the Hilton hotel chain for example; it has evolved into 10 different brands to serve people with different needs. It has designed hotels for people who prefer contemporary design with a luxury touch (Conrad), people who need a kitchen (Homewood Suites), people who need an extended stay (Home2), and has even created a separated brand for value conscious traveler (Hampton). The list goes on and on… Perhaps the one that I like the most is the DoubleTree hotel as it serves fresh baked cookies when you check in!

2. Save Money through Better Targeting of Your Customers

There are some other good reasons why you should implement market segmentation. In my opinion, segmentation makes marketing easier. A company can better target them by grouping customers who share similar needs and background together, you can better target them. Canada is a multi-cultural society and the one-size-fits-all approach may not be suitable. For example, in trying to target the Korean community in Toronto, instead of dropping direct mail pieces in all FSAs (forward-sorting areas) through Canada Post, the company can fine-tune its mailing list to target the Bloor/Bathurst and Yonge/Finch areas where the Koreans mostly reside.

3. Explore Untapped Business Opportunities

Secondly, by going through the market segmentation exercise, niche markets may be discovered and targeted. These may be underserved or even unserved markets that have specific needs. For example, CIBC forms a dedicated team to provide Aboriginal banking service to groups such as First Nations, Inuit, and Metis. The bank is doing that because it recognizes the unique banking needs of the aboriginal community.

4. Make Your Marketing Activities Relevant

The third good reason to divide customers into groups is to make the marketing process more efficient and relevant. Thinking of giving out free hockey tickets to new customers who buy your product? That may not be a good idea because not everybody in Canada likes to watch the Maple Leafs although it is a popular sport in this country. Through proper market segmentation, you can avoid sending the wrong marketing message or incentive to your customers.

5. Improve Profitability for Your Business

Finally and perhaps most importantly, companies use segmentation to improve their profitability. Major wireless such as Bell, Rogers, and TELUS also own discount brands namely Virgin Mobile and Solo, Fido and Chat-r, and Koodo respectively. These tier-2 brands are highly profitable because most of the network costs have already been absorbed by the primary brand. The use of subbrand helps to improve the network utilization overall for better ROI for the wireless companies. To ensure that cannibalization (loss of revenue owing to customers downgrading and using the cheaper service) does not happen, the selection of handset and rate plans is rather limited as compared to the primary brand.

Understand the Key Characteristics of a Market Segment

Before I show you all kinds of segments that you can identify, let us take a look at "how" these segments should be created. The following are some of the key criteria for segmenting a market:

1. **Each segment should be homogeneous (similar) within itself**. In other words, customers in the same segment should demonstrate similar characteristics and needs.

2. **Different segments should be heterogeneous (different) between themselves**. That is, each group of customers should have different needs with minimal overlap.

3. **Each segment should demonstrate measurable difference**. If you cannot tell their differences using traditional market research methods (survey, database mining.. etc) or there is a lack of such key information, just forget it. Sometimes privacy laws and regulations prevent you from asking your respondents certain questions (e.g. are you a HIV/AIDS patient?) thus not allowing segmentation at all.

4. **Segmentation should be justifiable financially**. Why bother to do the segmentation if the incremental profits obtained from the new segments are less than the cost of carrying out the segmentation exercise?

5. **Each segment should be durable**. I mean the customers' characteristics and needs should remain stable enough to exist over some planning horizon. Segmentation is not feasible if customers change their behavior or preference every week or so.

6. **Each segment should be large enough to be economically sustainable**. What is the purpose of having a segment with only a few people?

7. **Each segment should not only be identifiable but also actionable through segment profiling**. To illustrate the importance this point, let us consider the situation where you want to target those secret agents such as CIA or MI6. These segments cannot be found via interviews, surveys, or data mining. Even if these secret agents can really be located successfully, will they respond to invitations and present themselves in a product launch event or party later on? Not likely.

8. **Each segment should be accessible through regular media and distribution channels**. If your marketing message cannot be sent to your target customers and have them make purchases in the sales channel that you have access to, there is no point in having this segment. For example, it is a waste of time to find astronauts because they will not receive

direct mails or have time to visit your store for Boxing Day sales when working up in space.

Choose Number of Segments

How many customer segments should I have? This is a multi-million dollar question and there is no easy answer. Before jumping into the conclusion with a magical number, let us explore the different kinds of segmentation strategies that an organization can use. There are four major ones:

1. **Un-differentiation**: This means that the company does not target any specific market segment when operating the business. An example would be a gas station. When you drive your car to Petro-Canada for gasoline, can you get a discount because you are a student or a retired person? The price that you pay is very straightforward; your payment is based on the volume of gasoline you pump into your car. Also, you cannot get a faster service simply because you are driving a BMW or Mercedes-Benz. The gas station treats all customers relatively equally on a "first come, first served" basis. Although there are different grades of gasoline for drivers to select, there is no gas station chain that targets only American, Japanese, or German cars.

2. **Concentration** or **single niche**: This means that the company has one major target segment. Take Costco as an example, it targets those customers who are willing to buy in bulk to save money. Similarly, Rolls Royce targets a niche market in the high-end auto market and its cars are not suitable for everybody.

3. **Differentiation** or **multiple niches**: If a company is using this strategy, it usually has two or more segments to target. This is typical for a company that has operations across the country. For example, TELUS has some services (e.g., TELUS TV) that are available only in certain provinces in Canada. Therefore, their official web site requires the potential customer to select the province of residence at first instance of visit to their site. This strategy is common in the auto market where car manufacturers often make cars under different brand names to cater to the needs of various customers. For example, General Motor's Cadillac brand is targeting those matured customers who are looking for luxury, power, and style. Meanwhile, its Chevrolet brand is a mainstream line that has relatively good fuel efficiency with a well-balanced style and performance ratio.

4. **Atomization** or **customization**: This is the case when a company has dozens to thousands of segments. To implement atomization or customization, the company must be highly efficient in their operations because it often requires one-to-one marketing strategies. Take Dell for example; almost every order is different with a high level of customization. It can also be argued that Amazon.ca is following this approach as well because returned customers are presented with a list of suggested books based on their prior purchase pattern.

Reverting to our original question on number of segments, the organization's constraints (e.g., money, time, people skill-sets) and its business objectives (e.g., profits or revenue maximization? short-term or long-term goal?) have to be considered. Take the top Japanese car manufacturers as example; they only make use of two brands to serve its segments. Examples include Toyota/Lexus, Honda/Acura, and Mazda/Infiniti.

Having too many segments and associated brands can be risky especially if the organization does not have sufficient resources to support these segments in the long run. Air Canada has transformed its discount carrier, Tango, into just a fare class, whereas Ford has decided to discontinue manufacturing the Mercury brand from October 2010. A GM vehicle owner will be aware that the company has ceased manufacturing many brands including Hummer, Oldsmobile, Pontiac, and Saturn.

"A Priori" versus "Post Hoc" Segmentation Approach

There are two basic methodologies in carrying out segmentation. They are known as "A priori" and the "Post hoc" methods. "A priori" segmentation is usually carried out without primary research and involves analysis of secondary or historical data. In this kind of segmentation, both segmentation criteria and its definitions are defined "before" data collection. In other words, the number of segments and description are known in advance. For example, if you want to group the samples based on gender and residing province, you have to determine the segment details as in the following table prior to collecting the data:

Gender\Province:	BC	ON	Other Province
Male			
Female			

Once you have collected the data, all you need to do is to place each sample into the appropriate box based on the segmentation criteria. On the other hand, "Post hoc" segmentation often involves primary research. In this kind of segmentation, consumers' characteristics or their reactions to a new product or service are not known in advance. Hence, segments are not defined until "after" data is collected. To define the segments, statistical analysis procedures such as Cluster Analysis and/or Conjoint Analysis can be used.

To put it in very simple terms, post hoc segmentation is used because samples cannot be grouped accurately using pre-existing segmentation criteria such as demographic information only. As such, questions about customer's preferences on your topic of interest need to be asked, followed by a statistical analysis to determine if certain groups of people can be defined. Post hoc segmentation is also known as response-based segmentation because it often involves the use of surveys or interviews.

Segmentation Readiness Checklist

By now, you may be so excited that you want to start segmenting your customers immediately. Before you do so, calm down to see if you are actually ready to begin this segmentation exercise. Tevfik Dalgic and Maartin Leeuw have once created the following "Niche Marketing" readiness checklist that is applicable to those who intend to do segmentation in their organizations:

1. Do you know your firm's strengths, weaknesses, and competitive advantage?

2. Do you understand your customer, inside and out?

3. Is your company dependent on one or a limited number of customers? Do most of your sales come from a single product?

4. Have you developed an ongoing customer information system? Does it measure sales, profits, and market response links?

5. How well do you know your competition? (e.g., Why do customers use competitive products? How can you get them to switch?)

6. What is your positioning strategy? Have you developed and communicated a clear image for your product/product line? How is your product differentiated from your rivals'?

7. Have you created your own safe haven in the market? (Try not to compete with yourself, but create high-entry barriers for others.)

8. Are your resources spread too thin? (Watch for overexpansion, attacking too many niches.)

9. Is your marketing program synergistic? Is it consistent with your financial, management, operations, and R&D strategies?

10. Are you monitoring shifts in the marketplace and responding quickly to them?

In reality, most marketers would only say "Yes" to just a few of these questions. If you absolutely have no clue about your customers, your products, and the vision and missions of your organization, perhaps you should first spend some time to do your homework in these areas prior to initiating the segmentation exercise. If you feel you are ready for the challenge, then proceed to read the next few chapters to gain some ideas about the various segmentation strategies.

Chapter 4 - Basic Segmentation Examples for Consumer Market

Consumer Market—A Quick Definition

Some of my students somehow like to put an equal mark between the words "Consumer" and "Customer" but I think it is not too appropriate. This is because you can have a business customer (i.e., a commercial firm, a non-profit organization, or a government agency) who is not a consumer obviously. Hence, when I say the consumer market, I am referring to the residential market that includes consumers such as you and me.

In other words, consumers = residential customers = individual shoppers = you and me

How about small-office/home-office (SOHO)? No, even if you are running a one-person shop such as graphics designing at home, you are still part of the business market because you will have different decision-making considerations as compared to a typical consumer. In general, you can break down your consumer market in many ways. I will first discuss about some basic strategies one should have heard of, and then discuss some advanced ones that you can use to impress your boss or professor.

If you are looking for segmentation strategy for the business-to-business (B2B) market, please jump to read the latter part of this chapter.

Demographic Variables

You can break down your customers based on their Age, Gender, Income, Education, Occupation or Ethnicity in general.

Age

The use of demographic variables in segmentation is very common. McDonald's Happy Meal includes not only food in smaller portions but also a unique toy that keeps rotating from time to time. It is an attractive meal option for kids as it is less expensive than the regular combo, and I think it is a brilliant marketing tactic. That is because the kids rarely visit McDonald's alone and often come with their parents. Without such Happy Meals, some of these parents may not visit the restaurant otherwise. Furthermore, the kids may want to own not just one but a whole collection of toys; parents may therefore have to spend money at McDonald's multiple times.

Tips: At McDonald's, you can actually just buy the toy(s) without the purchase of a complete set of Happy Meals. If your kids are trying to collect a set of toys, just ask the cashier if they actually have them in stock. Although the restaurant is presenting just one style of toy for the week, they may actually have the rest of the toy styles for sale simultaneously.

When I was a university student, I once spent 3 hours on a Saturday morning to stand in a queue at the Hummingbird centre in downtown Toronto just to purchase the $10 theatre ticket. They call it the "tsoundcheck" tickets and one had to be between the ages of 15 to 35 to buy them. As I was financially down at that point in time, I could not afford the regular ticket fare at $80+. To me, getting the opportunity to watch a show was more important than selecting a good seat, plus I had plenty of free time back then! But why did the Toronto Symphony Orchestra (TSO) simply not sell the unsold tickets to students online or over the phone? Well, that is a tactic to avoid cannibalization. If cheap tickets are available easily, who would buy at regular fares? TSO has a highly painful strategy but this strategy is effective in attracting young people to watch TSO shows.

Ethnicity

Organizations are also creating products and services to suit the needs of certain ethnic groups. The banking sector has been remarkable in segmenting customers based on ethnicity. For example, TD Waterhouse has set-up a special hot-line with Chinese-speaking representatives, even as TD Bank's ATM machines can display localized languages (in addition to English and French) depending on the ATM's location.

Gender

In Canada, it is common to find fitness centres that target a certain gender. For example, Goodlife has women-only health clubs in selected locations. Is there health-clubs for men only? I know they exist in the States but I have not yet come across one in this country.

Geographic Variables

Marketer can group customers based on their location of residence in the country. Variables such as Country, City, Province, Postal Code, Field Sorting Area (FSA), Region (e.g. Western Canada vs Eastern Canada), or the type of city (e.g., Urban vs. Rural) can be used.

Does it matter?

Of course! Canada is a society comprising people from all walks of life. In fact, it can even be argued that Canada is composed of very different types of people who are loosely linked together. By grouping people by region, companies can better target their marketing efforts and reveal business opportunities they might have overlooked. In other words, people who are residing in different provinces often demonstrate very different needs. Have you ever tried the Slurpee drink at 7-Eleven? Generally, people drink significantly more pops or coffee than Slurpee in Canada. However, Manitoba is known as the Slurpee capital of the world! This is because Manitobans consumed over 188,000 Slurpee drinks per month, significantly more than the average from other Canadian provinces. If 7-Eleven is considering the average Slurpee consumption in Canada, it may be low as compared to other countries. However, if 7-Eleven is able to group consumers per region, it will realize that there is a huge market for Slurpee in Canada…with the highest market potential in Manitoba followed by Alberta.

Related stories:
http://www.winnipegfreepress.com/local/one-cool-city----slurpee-champs-yet-again-98094759.html
http://corp.7-eleven.com/AboutUs/FunFacts/tabid/77/Default.aspx

Psychographic Variables

Everybody is different in terms of his or her psychographic characteristics. A survey will rarely find two people having the same lifestyle, lifecycle, interest, attitudes, opinions, or values. Do spouses enjoy doing the same activity at home, such as watching the Hell's Kitchen TV show or reading the Maclean's magazine? It is possible occasionally but not all the times, right? People in general have their own preferences in life and marketers can leverage this information to group similar consumers together for better target marketing.

PART 3   Advanced Segmentation Techniques

Chapter 5—The Eight Mental Models of Segmentation for Consumer Market

Benefit Segmentation

By now, you should know about some basic ways to segment your consumer market. In the past few decades, marketers have explored other ways to divide a market. However, I can think of eight more ways to perform segmentation and one of them is called "Benefit Segmentation". There are all kinds of benefits that people seek. It includes physical benefits, emotional benefits, mental benefits, intellectual benefits, and spiritual benefits. How our needs can be filled directly affect how we perceive the value of a product or service.

Think about candles. To some people, candles are inexpensive item that should be bought from a dollar store or supermarket because its basic function is to give us light; you buy candles to put them on birthday cakes or use them when there is a power outage at home. Have you shopped at Chapters or Michael's lately? People are now buying beautiful candles at 10 times the price simply because of their smell and not necessarily for its light. Some people use these expensive candles as part of their "stress-relief" therapy. Some even argue that by removing the unpleasant odor in the office, people's work productivity can be increased too! These are the emotional and mental benefits that I am referring to.

Candle for stress relief?

With this understanding, the candle maker can generate significant amounts of revenue by different kinds of candles for different customer segments. It is no longer the width, length, or color that matters. The new questions when designing your candle become "What kind of benefits my product can bring and how much price premium this customer segment is willing to pay to enjoy these benefits?"

Other examples using benefit segmentation includes the Starbucks coffee shop that I have mentioned earlier in this book. Do people go to Starbucks simply to fix their caffeine needs? If it is just about getting good coffee at a great price, one could better go to Tim Hortons or Country Style. If you have ever been to Starbucks, you will realize that it is not just a coffee shop. It is a place for people to relax, listen to music, meet clients, read books, or type their homework assignments. To many sales people, Starbucks is their office on the road! To target customers in these benefit segments, what is more important to the coffee shop is its ambiance, the music it plays, and the wi-fi Internet connection rather than the selection of coffee beans for the day.

Some students have trouble understanding the meaning of physical benefits. How about those Rugged personal digital assistant (PDAs) that the courier delivery folks use and also those rugged laptops that are used by fire and law enforcement agencies?

Rugged laptop

Lifestyle and Lifecycle Segmentation

This segmentation strategy asks you to group customers not by their demographics characteristics, but by their psychological and personality differences. Take the credit card industry as example, how do you compete with the top four or five Canadian banks when you are a new player in town? The Bank of America has been successfully targeting school alumni and organization's members with its 3500+ kinds of white-label affinity credit cards in Canada. If you are holding a university alumni credit card, there is a good chance that you are actually a customer of MBNA, a subsidiary of Bank of America. This bank may not be able to sign you up as a credit card holder if they promote the card as a Bank of America credit card. By associating itself with organizations that you are proud of, and contributing to these organizations' success (in terms of sharing profits from the card), the bank has been growing successfully in Canada.

Credit card for the UofT community

Source: https://wwwa.applyonlinenow.com/CACCapp/Ctl/entry?sc=cc42&lc=en_CA

Another example that I can think of is the female-oriented Goodlife Fitness and medical clinic at selected Loblaws. The fact is that increasing numbers of female professionals are working long hours these days and they have no time to drive around after work. By having everything under one roof, Loblaws is able to capture customers who have busy lifestyles.

GoodLife Fitness Clubs for Women & Kids

Belief Segmentation

Do you have a strong perception towards a certain brand of product (or type of service) that prevents you from consumption? For example, some men will never go to a SPA because they think it is only for ladies, whereas others will not dine in a French restaurant because they believe it is so expensive that they will never be able to afford such a meal. Some consumers will not buy a particular brand simply because they do not believe that such brand can ever satisfy their needs, both functionally and mentally.

A marketer should identify growth opportunity among the non-users as part of the business growth strategy. A new product, a new image, or a trial opportunity can be developed that overcomes the objection of the consumers who have negative beliefs about your product or service, especially if the beliefs are wrong. Have you ever heard of the Summerlicious and Winterlicious events that take place in Toronto? They are organized by the City of Toronto to promote tourism. During these events, customers can enjoy a 3-course meal at a participating up-scale restaurant for just $25 to $45. These restaurants are trying to attract the non-belief customer segment to try their food. The rationale behind this strategy is that by getting the customer to try the fancy dishes at a price that he or she can afford during the limited time period may yield the following response: "Ah, this is a nice place. While we won't dine here regularly, perhaps we can come back to this restaurant for our anniversary or birthday celebration!"

Learn more about these events at:
http://www.toronto.com/winterlicious
http://www.toronto.ca/special_events/summerlicious/2010/index.htm

To further illustrate the importance of belief segmentation, let us consider those sales people who sell cosmetic products in those shopping mall kiosks or department store. What do they wear? Yes, they are wearing those "White color doctor's coat". But hey, they are neither doctors, pharmacists, nor nurses so why are they wearing that plain white coat?

Selling cosmetic in a store

The answer is very simple. Some consumers will only take the advise from a health professional seriously. If a sales person wears a T-shirt and a pair of blue jeans and say, "Madam, your skin is too dry and you need this $100 anti-wrinkle cream.", you may not pay too much attention as you may not trust this stranger. However, when this sales person is wearing the white coat, you may trust more of his or her advice as your brain has unconsciously categorized this sales person as a health care professional. The white coat gives you more confidence in the purchase. With this understanding, the shop can better target the non-believers.

Product Usage Segmentation

Another way to segment your market is to consider their behavior, such as usage level. Some people need to travel on the train regularly so VIA Rail has launched the "VIA 6 Pak" that saves these heavy-usage commuters up to 50% on regular fare. VIA Rail knows that mass marketing is not suitable to promote this ticket type because not everybody needs to commute on such routes that often. Hence, VIA Rail mainly advertises the "VIA 6 Pak" in college and university campus to target out-of-town students.

I can think of another example to better illustrate the use of product usage segmentation strategy. Do you drink Starbucks coffee? In the past, people mainly ordered their "Tall Bold" at the Starbucks cafe or bought packs of Starbucks ground coffee beans to brew coffee at home or office. Although Starbucks has been aggressively opening up new cafes across Canada, there are still places such as the Service Centres on Hwy 401 where you cannot find a Starbucks to get your caffeine fix. To satisfy the needs of these heavy Starbuck drinkers, a new product known as "Starbucks VIA Ready Brew" (it has nothing to do with the VIA Rail that has been just mentioned!) was launched in 2010. It is basically a pack of instant coffee powder and all you need is hot water to make your Starbucks coffee on the road!

Choice Rule Segmentation

Some people are highly logical when it comes to shopping. They may compile a spreadsheet to analyze the pros and cons of buying certain brands and may even enquire at three or more stores prior to spending the dollars. To them, the return on investment (ROI) is the key. We refer to them as consumers who demonstrate "logical choice behavior". On the other hand, some people are not that rational or logical when they shop. They are willing to spend the money whenever they feel good about themselves, the shop, the product, or when it is a beautiful sunny day. These consumers are not interested in the nitty-gritty of the product features and they often purchase when they are in good mood. We refer to them as consumers who demonstrate "experiential choice behavior".

With this understanding, a marketer has to ask this question, "What kind of customer is my brand likely to attract? Is it the rational or the irrational one?" Once your target market's profile is known, the marketing mix should be adjusted accordingly. Comparatively speaking, people who buy Windows-based PCs are usually rational ones. That is why in your local computer paper or magazines, you will often find PC advertisements showing those highly detailed (and complicated) product specifications comparing different kinds of PCs, in terms of CPU speed, bus speed, cache size, and all those highly technical features. On the contrary, people who buy Apple Macs in general are comparatively less rational. Some buy the Macs because "It's cool to use a Mac", "I like the white color", "I just want a computer that works with no virus", or even "I love Steve Jobs!". Hence, Apple's advertisement rarely focuses on its product specifications but rather paints a great picture why you should get a Mac from the usability and brand positioning perspectives.

Brand Loyalty Segmentation

Another way to look at your customers is from their degree of loyalty to your brand. Some consumers are very proud of the brands that they have chosen and always want to tell the world that they are part of the brand. Honda's advertisement always focuses on the "team" element and shows off "street racing" on TV commercials. The company is also the title sponsor of the Toronto and Edmonton Indy races. This attracts those car buyers who may want to join the Honda family to share the racing job, even if they are not street racers themselves. Just searching the web yields many active Honda user groups and forums. Similar is the situation with the Mazda brand. If you whisper "zoom-zoom" in the office and your next door colleague replies with a "zoom-zoom", you know he or she is also a Mazda driver. That is the language that is being spoken in the Mazda family and their TV advertisements reinforce this message.

Learn more at:
http://www.mazda.com/mazdaspirit/zoom-zoom/

So, what should a company do to their loyal customers who really like the brand? Get them together and build the cult! Turn these customers into brand ambassadors. Harley-Davidson often holds barbecue (BBQ) events at the local dealerships. Every year, Harley-

Davidson riders come together to drive across the country during summertime I believe. These relationship-building activities are good ways to increase your brand stickiness. That is why Honda motorcycle riders rarely switch to become a Harley-Davidson one and vice versa.

Other brands such as Jimmy Choo, Nike, and Tim Hortons all made use of the brand loyalty segmentation strategy to increase their customer base even as retaining existing ones. Just ask a Tim Hortons coffee lover, he or she will give so many reasons why Tim's coffee is way better than those of Second Cup, Starbucks, and Bridgehead.

Jimmy Choo shoes

In other words, do special things (from the marketing perspective) for your loyal customers because they have different needs than others. Help them "love" your brand; they will pay back by buying more of your goods in the future, or promote that brand through word-of-mouth in their networking circles.

Price Sensitivity Segmentation

The idea about price sensitivity is very straightforward: some consumers are not willing to pay any price premium and they do not mind receiving a reduced set of service. On the other hand, there are consumers who do not mind paying a bit extra to get better services. These two groups of consumers are highly distinctive and they will not change their consumer behavior easily even if they get higher or lower income.

This explains the reason why companies launch different brands to target customers who have different price sensitivity. Take the department store Hudson Bay Company (the Bay) as an example; do you know that it also operates the Zellers to target the value-conscious shoppers? Similarly, the bank CIBC operates President's Choice Financial to target those customers who enjoy "No fee banking". In the retail side, the GAP operates Banana Republic on the high-end side and Old Navy in the value-shopper segment.

So, what does it mean to the marketer? If the company is selling a wide range of products with very different price points, perhaps it is time to open a separate brand to target those value shoppers and/or those with high disposable incomes. Some consumers just feel uncomfortable shopping at Holt Renrew because it is out of their league, even if the store is running a 80% discount super summer sale! Of course, it really depends on the organization's objective and available resources. This is because operating multiple brands means doubling if not tripling of your resources.

Search and Shopping Segmentation

The travel industry is a good example to explain how people select their hotels. Of course, there are different features among Hilton, Holiday Inn, Marriott and Delta but to some people, these three- or four-star hotels are just the same with minor differences.

Some people like to read the Travel section in their Toronto Star newspaper to learn about goods vacation deals, whereas others only rely on the web to get the latest offerings. My dad is a great example of people who neither surf the web nor reading the English newspaper. Whenever he wants to go for a vacation and needs advice, he walks into the local travel agency and talks to his favorite travel agent, Robert. See, people utilize different kinds of channels to search for the product or service that they want. Some people only buy books online because they are fed up with the limited book selection at the physical store. Meanwhile, there are others who would only buy leather jackets or shoes in those outlets as they often feel buying at regular retailers is a bad financial transaction.

The point that I am making is that consumers have very different search behavior and shopping styles. My students are now buying e-books online and downloading songs on their cell phones. Hence, marketers need to explore these new sales and advertising channels or else a large chunk of customers may be missed. Companies are advertising on redflagdeals.com to capture those tech-savvy online shoppers; have you considered this advertising channel?

If you are old enough, I guess you still remember this retail chain called "Consumers Distributing". It went bankrupt in the late 1990s because people no longer wanted to visit the store in person to place a mail-order. When you can shop online comfortably from home, Consumers Distributing's business model suddenly becomes irrelevant!

Chapter 6—Consumer Segmentation Framework Developed by Commercial Firms

P-Types

In Canada, one of the popular methods for segmenting the consumer market is developed by Martin Goldfarb of the Goldfarb Consultants. It is commonly known as the "P-Types" which stands for Psychographic Types.

Unlike other popular segmentation methodologies, Goldfarb's approach focuses on segmenting consumer attitudinally instead of considering their demographic or behavioral characteristics. By studying consumers' attitudes and values, this segmentation method not only helps marketers to match the product offerings and company image with the right kind of consumers using the product, but also helps them to fine tune their marketing message in promotion and customer relationship management activities. With a good understanding of their customer's psychographic characteristics, marketers can better attract new customers and retain key ones. Based on factor and cluster analysis of 300 survey questions answered by Canadians from 1999 to 2001, nine distinctive segments in the Canadian consumer market have been identified:

- Disinterested Outsiders (5%)
- Tie-Dyed Grey (9%)
- Passive Malcontents (14%)
- Les "Petite Vie" (12%)
- Protective Providers (11%)
- Contented Traditionalists (14%)
- Joiner Activists II (13%)
- Mavericks (9%)
- Up and Comers (13%)

I will describe each of these consumer segments in the following pages

Disinterested Outsiders

About 5% of the Canadians are suggested to fall into the "Disinterested Outsiders" consumer category. These consumers are found to be apathetic, show little concern for others, and do not care much about ethical behavior. To some extent, disinterested outsiders are materialistic and not career-oriented. They feel uncomfortable with high-tech gadgets and often require assistance from others. This group of consumers is usually under 35 years old, have lower household income and likely not married. So, what does it mean if your customers are disinterested outsiders? To attract them to buy your product or service, you need to

1. Use deep discounts and aggressive promotion
2. Make sure financing or payment deferment is available
3. Explicitly spell out the good reasons to buy your product
4. Avoid using too much hype or buzz in communication

Tie-Dyed Grey

About 9% of Canadians belong to the "Tie-Dyed Grey" consumer segment. These consumers are observed to hold liberal and progressive attitudes, enjoy being alone, and are not materialistic. Tie-Dyed Grey are interested in national and international events, and they have relatively lower respect for government authority and corporations. This group of consumers is often older, retired and speak English as their primary language. It is also found out that Tie-Dyed Grey are often not married and they like to live in cities more than in rural areas. So, what does it mean if your customers are Tie-Dyed Grey? To attract them to buy your product or service, you need to

1. Avoid family-focus or romantic positioning
2. Use simple English instructions for product installation and avoid technology jargon
3. Focus on "in-person" support at the retail level
4. Provide after-sale service
5. Use live operators instead of interactive voice recognition (IVR) system for phone service

Passive Malcontents

About 14% of Canadians are "Passive Malcontents". These consumers are found to be passive, lonely, lead a solitary life, and unhappy with their personal life in general. They lack self-confidence but trust others especially the government. This group of consumers are old, retired, and probably not in the labor force anymore. They also love their country and demonstrate strong patriotism. "Passive Malcontents" speak English as their primary language and less likely to have children at home. So, what does it mean if your customers are "Passive Malcontents"? To attract them to buy your product or service, you need to

1. Promote how your product or service can enhance their appearance or feeling
2. Provide home delivery or in-house service
3. Provide longer product warranty to give peace of mind
4. Use local manufacturers to make products as much as possible. If possible, make your product locally to have the "Made In Canada" status.
5. Make sure your product is simple to set up and use Health concerns – but must require minimal effort and expense
6. Focus on customer loyalty program

Les "Petite Vie"

About 12% of the Canadians are suggested to fall into the "Les Petite Vie" consumer category. These consumers are found to be deliberate, very social in their small circle of friends, and have strong views on crime and violence in the society. To some extents, "Les Petite Vie" are slow paced and they feel uncomfortable with change. They are followers and not a leader. This group of consumers is mostly French Canadian (80%). They are female, live in small towns, and have low household income in general. So, what does it mean if your customers are "Les Petite Vie"? To attract them to buy your product or service, you need to

1. Focus on word-of-mouth referral and TV advertising
2. Leverage a trusted spokesperson for your brand or product
3. Avoid the "New and Improved" positioning
4. Leverage well-known brand names, or focus on brand building activities
5. Emphasize the history and rationale behind your brand
6. Make your customers believe that your product, your brand, and your organization are here to stay

Protective Providers

About 11% of the Canadians are "Protective Providers". These consumers are family focused, hard working, proud of their own achievements, and respect law and order. To some extents, "Protective Providers" demonstrate some financial concerns and they do not trust the politicians too much. They are often young, married, and parents of small children. This group of consumers is relatively less well-educated and is a blue collar worker. So, what does it mean if your customers are "Protective Providers"? To attract them to buy your product or service, you need to

1. Provide them with best value for money
2. Make sure long-term financing arrangements and special deals are available
3. Focus on brand building activities as they care about the brand
4. The product is durable and safe to use
5. Ensure there are no financial surprises (e.g. extra fees) when using your product

Contented Traditionalists

About 14% of Canadians belong to the "Contented Traditionalists" consumer category. In general, these consumers are happy, family-oriented, and not selfish. "Contented Traditionalists" hold traditional moral values and have good religious foundation. The majority of this group is female (71%) and they are married with children. Many "Contented Traditionalists" are also homeowners. So, what does it mean if your customers are "Contented Traditionalists"? To attract them to buy your product or service, you need to

1. Stress old-time values and heritage/history of your brand
2. Show how your product or service can bring family togetherness
3. Show how your product or service can improve the customers' education and healthy living style.
4. Provide a total, hassle-free, full-service such as delivery, installation, and maintenance
5. Remind customers about the benefits of being your customers

Joiner Activists II

Approximately 13% of Canadians falls into the "Joiner Activists II" consumer category. They are interested in political issues, are intellectually curious, and hold liberal values. The "Joiner Activists II" have concerns about the environment and have no religious background. This group of consumer often has high income, married with children and is well educated. They prefer to live in the city rather than rural areas. Very often, these consumers are willing to try new products and are early adopters. So, what does it mean if your customers are "Joiner Activists II"? To attract them to buy your product or service, you need to:

1. Use the "New Experience" positioning
2. Sell uniquely designed product or service
3. Focus on product or service quality
4. Use a sophisticated and intelligent tone in your marketing message
5. Act socially responsible
6. Provide them with detailed product or service information

Mavericks

About 9% of the Canadians are found to be "Mavericks". These consumers are found to be confident, individualistic, and risk-taking. They are forward thinking in terms of technology. "Mavericks" are voracious consumers and they are willing to pay their dream products or services. They are also leaders and early adopters. This group of consumers is mostly male (74%) and employed. They have high household income in general. So, what does it mean if your customers are "Mavericks"? To attract them to buy your product or service, you need to:

1. Leverage the Internet channel for communication
2. Provide them with fast and powerful high-tech products
3. Provide them with choices and
4. Give them the ability for product or service customization
5. Make them feel empowered

Up and Comers

About 13% of the Canadians are found to fall into the "Up and Comers" consumer category. They are ambitious and materialistic, but not intellectually curious. This segment of customers is outgoing and active and they hold traditional moral values. "Up and Comers" are young, often under 35 years old. They have high household income and do not mind paying for the latest gadgets and toys. "Up and Comers" are often first generation Canadians. So, what does it mean if your customers are "Up and Comers"? You can try to

1. Target them for entertainment and sports-related products
2. Focus on brand development, as reputation is important to them
3. Develop upscale, good taste advertisement
4. Reassure their social status
5. Help customers to increase their sense of self-worth with your product or service

VALS-Types

Whereas the P-Types has been popular in Canada, many marketers also make use of the Values, Attitudes, and LifeStyles (VALS)-Types to segment their customers as well. It is a segmentation methodology created by a company called Strategic Business Insights (previously known as SRIC-BI). The VALS method segments U.S. adults into eight types using a specific set of psychological traits and key demographics that drive consumer behavior.

The segmentation involves participants to complete a 40-question VALS Survey to understand if they are primary motivated by ideals, achievement or self-expression. Their available resource and level of innovation are also considered. The eight VALS-Types are:

Consumers who are mainly motivated by Ideals, Achievement and Self Expression:
- **Innovators**

Consumers who do not have any primary motivation:
- **Survivors**

Consumers who are mainly motivated by Ideals:
- **Thinkers**
- **Believers**

Consumer who are mainly motivated by Achievement:
- **Achievers**
- **Strivers**

Consumers who are mainly motivated by Self-Expression:
- **Experiencers**
- **Makers**

This VALS survey (free-of-charge, as of this writing) can be accessed from Strategic Business Insights' web site:

http://www.strategicbusinessinsights.com/vals/surveynew.shtml

(Note: if the link is broken, just go to their company's main web page and follow the links there)

Once the survey is completed, each participant will be identified with both a primary and secondary type. In other words, these VALS-types are not mutually exclusive in reality as consumer characteristics may overlap to a certain degree. It is all about which segment of people belong to it more.

Innovators

Innovators, as the name implies, are people who welcomes new ideas and technologies. They are change leaders, with high self-esteem, and capable of taking charge in the office. This consumer segment is motivated by ideals, achievement and also self-expression. They have high resources and high level of innovations. As Innovators have sufficient resources, they are active consumers and like to consume upscale and niche products and services. So, what does it mean if your customers are Innovators? To attract them to buy your product or service, you need to

1. Associate a positive and perhaps "cool" image with your brand
2. Focus on how your product promotes good taste, independence and personality
3. Show how your product or service is related to the personal or professional challenges that they are seeking
4. Give them lots of options to choose from.

Survivors

Unlike Innovators who are motivated by ideals, achievement, and self-expression, Survivors are in the other end of the spectrum without showing any strong primary motivation. As this group of consumers has very limited resources, they live a narrowly focused live and their primary concerns are in the area of personal safety, food, and security in general. These are the people who care more about their "needs" than "wants". Because of the narrowly focused lives that they are living in, Survivors are not interested in innovative approaches or solutions. What they want is predictability and familiarity. So, what does it mean if your customers are Survivors? To attract them to buy your product or service, you need to

1. Be modest in your product or service positioning as they are cautious consumers
2. Make use of price discounts and sales promotions to get them into your shops
3. Be straightforward about your product or service offerings, with simple unique selling propositions
4. Ensure the same product or brand is available in your store. If you are in the service industry, try to have the same group of staffs serving them

Thinkers

In general, you can consider Thinkers as people who are well educated and mature. They value knowledge, are open to new ideas, and often look for information in their decision-making process. Perhaps you can say these are logical shoppers. This group of customers is relatively happy and feels comfortable with what they are doing. Thinkers also have more resources relatively speaking. To enhance their knowledge, Thinkers like to read news about the world and they seek opportunity to broaden their knowledge. So, what does it mean if your customers are Thinkers? To attract them to buy your product or service, you need to

1. Give them some but not too many options to choose from
2. Be practical in your product or service positioning. Do not make empty promises
3. Show how durable your product is
4. Promote the functionality and good value in your product or service

Believers

Similar to Thinkers, Believers are also motivated by ideals but they lack the abundant resources that Thinkers have. These consumers are conservative people who hold traditional moral values and often have solid religious background. They care about their family, community, and the country in general. Believers like routines and high predictability. So, what does it mean if your customers are Believers? To attract them to buy your product or service, you need to

1. Try to associate your product offerings or promotion with their family, religion, community, and the nation
2. Focus on brand development
3. Focus on customer loyalty program
4. Avoid sudden changing of product or service offerings without proper consultation with these customers

Achievers

Achievers, as the name has indicated, are people who have personal or business goals to achieve. They have many wants and needs and are active shoppers. This group of consumers often makes deep commitment to their family and job or profession. They like to "get things done" and their social lives are structured around family, office, and churches. Politically speaking, Achievers are conservative; they respect local authority and also value consensus and stability in general. So, what does it mean if your customers are Achievers? To attract them to buy your product or service, you need to

1. Focus on prestigious brand positioning
2. Associate your product or service to their professional success and achievement
3. Show how your product or service can save them time or do things more efficiently
4. Generate brand awareness in their circle with repeat advertising

Strivers

Similar to Achievers, Strivers are also motivated by achievements but they lack the abundant resources that Achievers have. They often measure success with the money that they earn. Although Strivers are trendy, they are concerned about how others perceive them. This segment of consumer often lacks the skill-sets and focus required to be successful in their professional life. So, what does it mean if your customers are Strivers? To attract them to buy your product or service, you need to

1. Provide them with stylish products or services to make them look rich.
2. Help them to show off to their peers
3. Make good use of timing in the month to stimulate their purchase intentions
4. Make expensive products or services available to them once in a while, as they may be able to afford them sometimes

Experiencers

Experiencers are consumers who are mainly motivated by self-expression. They are young, enthusiastic, very active, and like to be "cool" in their circle of friends. Experiencers have sufficient resources and are impulsive consumers. They get excited about a new product or trend easily, even if some risks have to be taken. This consumer segment likes to spend money on high-end fashion and socializing. So, what does it mean if your customers are Experiencers? To attract them to buy your product or service, you need to

1. Sell them trendy, good-looking products
2. Invite them to try new product or services
3. Promote your brand in places where they hang out, such as fitness centres, sports arena, recreation center, and pubs
4. Focus on brand positioning; it has to be "cool"

Makers

Similar to Experiencers, Makers are also motivated by self-expression but they lack the abundant resources that Experiencers have. Instead of buying cool stuffs to show off, these consumers like to show off what they have created, for example, raising a child, fixing a computer, or as simple as cooking a delicious meal. Makers are practical and they like to acquire skills to improve upon themselves. This group of consumers lives in traditional family and has regular jobs. Although makers often respect government authority, they do not like their privacy to be intruded. So, what does it mean if your customers are Makers? To attract them to buy your product or service, you need to

1. Protect their privacy rights
2. Be moderate when introducing new products or services to them; probably need to help them understand why the new one is better
3. Focus on the practical functionality of your product
4. Sell them basic goods and service with great ROI

Chapter 7—Segmentation Examples for Business Market

Firmographic Segmentation

In the previous chapters, I have shown how a consumer market can be divided into groups. Now, let us turn our attention to the business market. You may have heard about terms such as "Firmographic segmentation" or "Firmographics"; they basically refer to ways that marketers use to group companies together based on their characteristics.

Before introducing the various segmentation strategies for the business market, I would like to stress once again the importance of checking your available resources to see if segmentation is really needed. Business customers are broken down into various groups because the company thinks it can serve the customer better by adjusting marketing mix (4Ps). If, the company is planning to sell the same product or service to the business customers using the same pricing, promotional, and channel strategies, then why bother with segmentation in the first place? Another point to recap is about the number of segments that should be created. If the company does not have the time to manage and support the segments, even three segments may be too much for the organization! More is not always better.

If the company still believes that it can serve its customers better by grouping them into different segments, please keep reading on. I am going to present some common strategies to segment the business market.

Employee Size

A basic way to segment business customers is to consider their number of employees. Although the exact employee number range may vary slightly depending on whom you ask, the majority of marketers would agree that companies can be grouped into the following types:

Number of employees:	Company Type:
A company with hundreds or more of employees working in different countries	Multi-national Corporation (MNC)
500 or above	Large Business, Corporation or Enterprise
100 to 499	Medium-sized Business
499 or lower	Small to Medium Enterprise (SME) or Small to Medium Business (SMB)
99 or lower	Small Business [if producing products]
50 or lower	Small Business [if providing service]
1 to 5	Micro-business or SOHO (Small office, Home Office)

Although employee size is one of the easiest ways to group companies together, it may not give marketers the best picture of business opportunity. This is because some companies, especially those operating in the graphics design, IT consulting, and web hosting sectors, only have a few people working in the office. A three-people web hosting company may seem to be a small operation, but it may require computer servers that cost millions of dollars and business Internet services that cost several thousand dollars a month! Do not let the employee numbers fool you particularly if you are not familiar with the industry that you are interested in selling to.

Size of Transaction

In addition to using employee size, measuring business customers based on their size of transaction can also be considered. Focus on the annual revenue and not profitability as the latter varies based on too many numbers of underlying factors. There are no clear rules in determining how business customers should be grouped based on revenue. Some companies use the million-dollar mark as the annual revenue cutting point, whereas others use a smaller scale. It really depends on the industry. Although the use of transaction size can seem easy, it can actually be difficult to find out especially if your business customers are small and medium businesses (SMBs) or are private companies that do not report its annual revenue to the public.

Standard Industrial Classification Code

In North America, one of the traditional ways to group companies together is to make use of a coding scheme called the SIC code. It stands for Standard Industrial Classification code which is a 4-digit code. For example, 2020 means manufacturer of dairy products, 2111 is maker of cigarette, and 7311 is advertising agencies. It covers both the manufacturing and service sectors.

So, why should I identify and group my business customers using the SIC code? One of the practical uses is the sourcing of mailing list from those data providers such as Dun & Bradstreet (D&B), InfoUSA, and Scott's Directories. When buying these lists for prospecting, the SIC code(s) you are looking for has to be clearly informed. Telling them to send a list of agriculture goods producers will be too generic.

The SIC Code has been use since the late 1930s and it is still commonly used by some government agencies such as the U.S. Securities and Exchange Commission. However, SIC has gradually been replaced by a newer system called the North American Industry Classification System (NAICS) code that was introduced in the late 1990s.

To view the full list of SIC code, visit these two pages:

http://www.statcan.gc.ca/subjects-sujets/standard-norme/sic-cti/sice-ctie80_menu-eng.htm

http://www.statcan.gc.ca/subjects-sujets/standard-norme/sicc-ctic/sicc-ctic80_menu-eng.htm

North American Industry Classification System Code

NAICS is the newer way to classify organizations. It stands for North American Industry Classification System. This 6-digit code is considered to be more detailed and comprehensive than the SIC codes that have been used for decades. For example, the NAICS code for Internet Service Provider is 518111. One of the interesting things about NAICS is that its codes are revised every 5 years. So, you may find more codes in the 2007 version of NAICS than those of 2002. Statistic Canada publishes information about these changes on its web site for the public to look up. See more at:

http://www.statcan.gc.ca/subjects-sujets/standard-norme/concordances/t2007_1-eng.htm

(If the link is broken, just go to the StatCan web site and search for NAICS under the "Definitions and Documentations" section)

To see the full list of NAICS code online, visit:

http://www.statcan.gc.ca/subjects-sujets/standard-norme/naics-scian/2007/list-liste-eng.htm

International Standard Industrial Classification of All Economic Activities Code

Whereas NIC and NAICS codes are North American focused, there is a coding scheme called ISIC that is often used as well. It stands for International Standard Industrial Classification and this 4-digit coding system is developed by the United Nations. For example, the ISIC code for provider of recorded media reproduction is 1820. To learn more about ISIC, please visit the following United Nation web page:

http://unstats.un.org/unsd/cr/registry/regcst.asp?Cl=27

The complete 2008, revision 4 edition of the ISIC code can be downloaded at:

http://unstats.un.org/unsd/cr/registry/isic-4.asp

Organizational Type

If you find the SIC, NAICS, and ISIC codes to be too complicated, perhaps you can simply group your business customers based on their role in the supply chain. For example, are they acting as manufacturers, wholesalers, or retailers? If your customers' organizational objective is not to make profits, you can group them into the "Non-Profit organization" category. Examples of nonprofits include the Red Cross, Universities, and YMCA. You can also set up a separate category as government if you are selling to municipal, provincial, or federal government agencies.

Buying Centralization

Some multinational corporations (MNCs) have subsidiaries around the world but the decision-marking process may not done locally in the country, so these countries have to be grouped together in a manner where each segment has its own authority to make purchase decision. For example, one segment may be called North America (which covers Canada, USA, and Mexico), whereas another segment may be called EMEA (which covers various countries in Europe, the Middle East and Africa). In Asia, you may hear a term called "Greater China" which includes not just China but also Hong Kong and Taiwan. In Europe, the term "Benelux" is a collective word referring to Belgium, the Netherlands and Luxembourg.

For illustrative purpose, let us say Canon wants to sell photocopiers to Apple Netherlands; Canon has to sell its proposal not directly to the country manager of Apple Netherlands, but to the purchasing director at Apple Benelux. But because Canon is going to talk to Apple Benelux which manages these three countries, Canon should put together a single proposal to sell photocopying solutions that covers Apple's operations in these three countries.

Location: Province and Regional Levels

Related to buying centralization is the use of actual geographical areas to segment your business customers. In Canada, you often find organizations grouping their business customers into three or four geographical segments, such as:

Western Canada - it covers British Columbia, Alberta, Saskatchewan and Manitoba.

Central Canada - Ontario and Quebec

Eastern Canada - it covers New Brunswick, Newfoundland and Labrador, Nova Scotia, Ontario, Prince Edward Island and Quebec

Atlantic Canada or **Maritime province** - it covers Nova Scotia, New Brunswick, and Prince Edward Island.

Northern Canada - it covers Yukon, Northwest Territories and Nunavut

Of course, some companies like to group their business customers by their provinces (or location of their headquarters), such as Alberta, Ontario, Manitoba…etc.

Location: City Levels using CMA, Postal Code, and FSA

Some organizations need to target SMBs in a large city (say Vancouver or Toronto) and they would make use of CMA, Postal Code, or FSA to help them. CMA stands for Census Metropolitan Area, a geographical unit that is developed and defined by Statistics Canada. Each CMA must have at least 100,000 residents in it. The area covered by the CMA can be different from those defined politically. For example, the Toronto CMA contains a large portion of the Greater Toronto Area but they are not the same. Learn more at:

http://www12.statcan.ca/english/census01/products/reference/dict/geo009.htm

Postal Code is a 6-digit code created by Canada Post to identify posting delivery areas. For example, the University of Toronto's main St. George campus has a Postal Code of M5S 1A1. As there are over 850,000 postal codes in Canada and each postal code covers a tiny block or two in the community, companies may want to step back to target a slightly larger area. This is where FSA comes in handy. FSA stands for Forward Sortation Area and it refers to the first three digits of a postal code. See the web site of Canada Post to learn more about postal code, FSA, and their geographical coverage:

http://www.canadapost.ca/cpc2/addrm/hh/current/indexp/cpALL-e.asp

PART 4   Creating Stickiness

Chapter 8—Product Differentiation

Importance of Product Differentiation

As I have pointed out earlier in this book, attracting customers to choose your product or service is an important step right after market segmentation in the 4-stage CRM process. So, what can you do to attract potential customers or get existing customers to buy more of your goods and services? In the last decade, the strategy of product differentiation has helped many organizations to achieve this goal. Therefore, I am writing this chapter to explain what it is and how you can do it.

Product differentiation has gained the attention of marketers because they have realized that this strategy helps to lower customer's price sensitivity. Here I am using the term customer because product differentiation can be applied to both consumer and business markets. Specifically, the more distinct the brand positioning and product performance on dimensions desired by the customer segment, the lower the price sensitivity of the segment will become. In other words, your customers will be more willing to pay the price premium if your product or service is very unique.

Take Apple's iPod as example. Is it a MP3 player? If you ask the Apple fans, they will probably say, "No, it's not a typical MP3 player! It's different!". They will praise the unique Apple design such as iPod's circular scroll wheel, user-friendly iTune interface, super-light weight, and most importantly the wide range of colors that they can choose from to match their mood and personalities. To reinforce their product differentiation, Apple has intentionally made its headphone in white color. Prior to Apple's iPod launch, virtually all of the MP3 Players in the market included those boring looking, black-color headphones. Now, when somebody who is wearing a white color headphone walks by, a good guess is that he or she is using an Apple product!

Relevancy of Product Attributes

Before you start to think about changing your product or service, let us see what makes a successful product differentiation. In my opinion, successful differentiation requires distinguishing a product (or brand) from its major competitors on an attribute that is meaningful and valuable to customers. What is interesting is that such an attribute (being uniquely different from others) can be relevant or totally irrelevant to the customers. My students will usually put up their hands at this moment because they are not sure about the 'irrelevancy' part. A quick example can illustrate this point.

Still remember the Influenza A virus (H1N1) pandemic that bothered many people around the word in 2009? Leveraging people's fear about this sickness, there is a Japanese clothing company called "Haruyama Trading Company" that launched the world's first Anti-H1N1 Swine flu Suit. According to this garment manufacturer, this suit is covered with titanium dioxide that reacts in sunlight to kill off the flu virus. The Japanese media has reported that people were queuing up on the street to buy this uniquely designed men's suit. However, if you ask any family physician, they will all tell you that the best way to fight with this flu is to wash your hands often using proper antiseptics, and avoid going to crowded places such as shopping malls and theaters. If these precautionary measures are not adopted, this innovative Anti-H1N1 suit will not do too much good to prevent contracting the flu. In fact, Samsung was one of the early pioneers in this area. In the mid-2000s where the H5N1 Avian flu was affecting Asia, Samsung introduced the SGH-E640 model mobile handset. It is unique because it claimed that the silver nano coating on the cell phone provides users with antibacterial protection.

Here is a side question: which place has more germs?
(a) Your toilet seat
(b) Your PC keyboard

The answer? It is (b). That's right, the keyboard that you use everyday in the office has way more germs than the toilet seat in the washroom! Again, if you don't wash your hands often, it does not matter if you are using your antibacterial cell phone or wearing a titanium dioxide coated suit!

So, are these companies stupid to create a unique selling proposition (USP) that is technically irrelevant? No, they are smart indeed. That is because a unique product or service will get the journalists' interest to talk about it more. Both of these products have been mentioned on TV, radio, and newspaper many times. The fact is that being different makes a brand more memorable and people will choose a more memorable brand more frequently. Not to mention that free publicity that these companies receive simply because of these news reporting. See, I am talking about them in my book so I am giving them free advertising as well.

3 Approaches to Product Differentiation

Now, you are interested in creating a product or service that is very different from your competitors, so where do you start? From my experience, companies utilize one or more of the following tactics for product differentiation, they are:

1. Physical differences
2. Perceived differences
3. Support service differences

I am going to give you some examples to illustrate these tactics.

Physical Differences

How much is your umbrella? $8, $15, or $20? How about a Dutch-designed umbrella that withstands wind speeds of up to 70 Mph? Yes, a typical Senz umbrella is selling for CAD$60 to CAD$100 depending on the size. This product is charging a price premium because it is one of those umbrellas that can withstand strong wind. Not buying this concept? A look at the following product photo will show how different it looks from umbrellas that you have used before:

Senz Umbrella

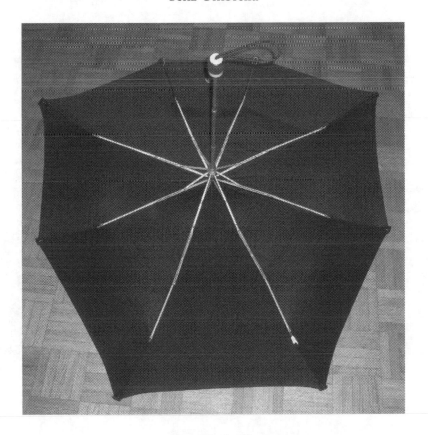

Senz Umbrella

One can easily differentiate Senz umbrella from other umbrella brands easily because of the asymmetrical design. This unique (or should I say strange?) umbrella design reinforces Senz' product positioning—protecting you from web during heavy rain and windy situations.

I can also think of another good example. What kind of materials are your credit card made of? 99.99% of the time, you will say "Plastic" if my guess is correct. Therefore, to differentiate its credit card from the rest, VISA makes use of "Carbon Graphite" to make its VISA Black Card —a specialized credit card that targets consumers who have very high purchasing power. It has the highest annual fee among all VISA cards at about US$495. This card is only available in selected countries and less than 1% of the population is qualified for applying this card. This is because you need to reach certain credit score and/or annual salary in order to obatain it. In other words, carrying a VISA Black Card is meant to symbolize personal or professional success. As I do not have a Black Card in my wallet (my TD First Class Travel Infinite VISA card does not count, although it is in black color!), I cannot really tell you how much satisfaction a carbon graphite card can bring to the cardholder as compared to a plastic one.

VISA Black Card

Source: https://www.blackcard.com/

Still not getting the concept of physical difference? I always save my best example last to ensure my students understand it. This example is Gillette's razors. When I first taught marketing, I asked my student this question "How many blades are there in a Gillette razor?" The answer was "two". Then, I asked if two blades were sufficient and most of the responses from the class were "Yes, but perhaps adding an extra one may make shaving faster." I repeated the questions throughout these years and the number of blades has gradually increased from two to five. So, is it really true that more blades in a razor will really give a better shaving experience? It does not matter if it is technically true or not, adding another blade to the razor seems to make the product a better one.

Gillette Fusion

Perceived Differences

The second way to differentiate your product is to create perceived differences. In other words, you are trying to make people to "think" that the new product feature is really important and hence the price premium is well justified. I am not saying that these newly created products do not have improvement over its original version, but does a 10% improvement justify a 40% price premium for example? I will let you to draw your own conclusion.

Pert Plus

The first product that I can think of is Proctor & Gamble's (P&G) Pert Plus 2-in-1. Why are people buying this shampoo plus conditioner combo instead of buying them separately? Common answers include "It's cheaper" and "I can wash my hair faster". Is it really true? Of course, it depends on the way you wash your hair but the reality is that you may not save that much money and washing time after all. To ensure you are willing to pay for the price premium and stick to this brand, P&G has created a whopping nine types of Pert Plus, namely:

- Pert Plus Moisturizing 3-in-1 (this is not a typo, it is 3-in-1)
- Pert Plus Light 2-in-1
- Pert Plus Medium 2-in-1
- Pert Plus Deep 2-in-1
- Pert Plus Fresh 2-in-1
- Pert Plus Dandruff Control 2-in-1
- Pert Plus Extra Body 2-in-1
- Pert Plus Color Care 2-in-1
- Pert Plus Dandruff Plus 2-in-1

See, there is always a Pert Plus product that fits your unique hair needs. What if one has dry extra body hair and suffers from dandruff problem? Some consumers may pick not just one but three bottles of Pert Plus from the shelf!

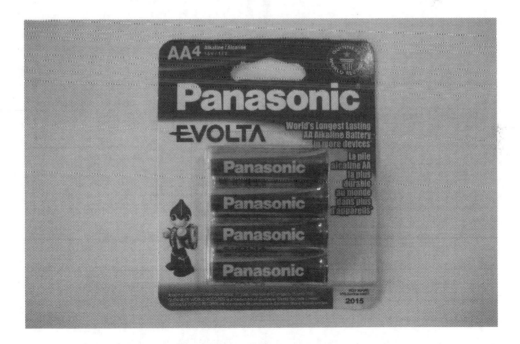

Panasonic Evolta Battery

Another example that I can think of is the Panasonic alkaline battery. When I was a small kid, there were only two types of consumer batteries: carbon zinc and alkaline. Now, the alkaline product category has many different kinds. Take Panasonic as example; it has the

"Evolta" line that claims to be recognized by GUINNESS WORLD RECORDS as the World's Longest Lasting AA Alkaline Battery Cell. Then, it has the "Digital Power" line that is designed for portable video games consoles and "Alkaline Plus" line for portable radio and pager. Similar to Panasonic, Duracell also create special batteries such as the "PowerPix" to target owners of digital camera. This product line uses something called "Nickel Oxy Hydroxide" and claims to be designed for digital camera uses. The camera photo on the right hand side of the packaging reinforces this product positioning.

Duracell PowerPix Battery

As you can see, there are different kinds of alkaline batteries designed for different devices. If your kids are asking you to buy some batteries for their CD players, portable video game consoles, digital camera, and digital clocks, how many kinds of these batteries are you going to buy? One, two or four? See, product differentiation is a good way to increase your revenue because consumers perceive that there is really a big difference among these products.

Another product that has been able to create huge perceived difference is Hewlett Packard's (HP) papers. In my opinion, there are only two kinds of papers; one for laser printer (including photocopiers) and one for printing colorful photos. However, it looks like HP has disagreed with me because they have created not just two but fifteen different kinds of papers to target different users. Technically speaking, papers have are defined by three attributes: size, weight and brightness. To show the differences among these HP papers, I am including their price points per 500 sheets, its paperweight in pounds, and also the brightness index in the parentheses.

HP Papers

- HP Office Paper ($5.39, 20/87)
- HP Multipurpose Paper ($6.95, 20/92)
- HP Office Recycled Paper ($7.28, 20/87)
- HP Printing Paper ($10.42, 22/92)
- HP Color Ink Jet Paper ($12.43, 24/100)
- HP Bright White Ink Jet Paper ($14.2, 24/108)
- HP Premium Ink Jet Paper ($69.12, 28/99)

- HP Laser Jet Paper ($12.83, 24/96)
- HP Premium Choice Laser Jet Paper ($23.03, 32/98)
- HP High Gloss Laser Paper ($157.40, 32/95)
- HP Photo Quality Ink Jet Paper, Matte ($115.15, 36/98)
- HP Photo Quality Ink Jet Paper, Semi-Gloss ($251.2, 89)
- HP Premium Photo Paper ($419.50)
- HP Premium Plus Photo Paper ($734.30)
- HP Premium Plus Photo Quality Ink Jet Paper ($786.25)

Support Services Differences

If you ask people what makes them remain loyal to a particular brand, you will often hear that it is all about great customer service. In today's competitive business environment, companies often focus on lowering their operating costs and make the mistake of thinking that customer service can be scarified, without realizing that providing good support service not only helps retain their customers, but also allow them to generate additional revenue in a post-sales situation.

The personal computer industry can be used to illustrate this point. In the 1980s and early 1990s, people liked to buy computers from their "mom and pop" computer store down the street. The market was filled with these locally assembled PCs because of its low prices. Although the PC was cheap, there was actually a problem that bothered many PC users: what could they do when their machine breaks down and who do they turn to for assistance? If lucky, you could possibly talk to the PC shop owner (who was often the tech guru) for help if he or she was not installing a PC elsewhere. Sure, you could leave your PC there and pay some extra fees for check up, but who knows when they would be ready for service? How about telephone support? Calling your local PC store at night or Sunday morning was futile as there would be no one to answer the phone calls. Although the "homemade PC" was cheap, this product did not address the support services that were required by most users who were not familiar with the technology.

That was why in early 2000s when all major PC manufacturers were launching those low-end models (e.g. Compaq's Presario) to target the mass consumer markets, many of these local PC shops terminated their businesses. This was because consumers were getting not just the PC itself but also the 24/7 technical support over the phone or via the Web. However, technical support at the retail level was still rather limited in the 2000s. Even with big brands such as Sony launching the Sony Style retail stores in shopping mall, most of these stores only facilitate as another sales channel or as "PC drop-off" location for repairs. "Restart your Windows" or "Reinstall your operating system" might be the only advice that you could get from these sales people.

Having a good understanding of this support service gap, Apple was able to attract many new customers by launching its own Apple Store. To the Mac users, the official Apple store is a great place because it has something called the Genius Bar, a section of the store that acts like your PC walk-in clinic. The Genius Bar is staffed with well-trained Mac technical gurus. Whether you are just having a quick question on how to use the iPhone, or need somebody to check out the cracked screen on your damaged MacBook, these Apple Genius (yes, that is their job title!) would be able to assist you right in the store. To serve customers better, Apple also allows online reservation of Genius Bar appointment and if you need extra personal care, you can sign up for an optional one-on-one computer consultation session that is charged by hour or incident.

Apple Genius Bar

If you compare the support service provided by various computer manufacturers, you will understand why a growing number of customers are choosing Apple products:

	24/7 Telephone Support	Online Forum Support	Retail Technical Support	One-on-One Consultation
Mom-and-Pop PC	No	No	Maybe	No
Dell	Yes	Yes	No	No
Apple	Yes	Yes	Yes	Yes

Another example that shows how support service can be used as a differentiation factor can be found in the credit card industry. If I ask you how many major kinds of credit card are there in the Canadian market, most people would say three, namely VISA, MasterCard, and American Express. But how about Diners Club card? Although Diners Club card carries a very high annual membership fee as compared to most credit cards on the market, and that it is less accepted than VISA in the retail market, it was able to attract certain customer segments especially in the business market. So, what makes Diners Club card so different from other cards?

To understand its unique selling proposition, one has to start with how your existing credit card is treating you. If my guess is correct, whenever you call up your credit card company to inquire about your account, the following situation will happen:

Card Company: Thanks for calling ABC Credit Card Company. For service in English, please press 1, for French, press 2...

You: Press 1.

Card Company: To serve you better, please enter your 16-digit credit card number and then press the # sign.

You: Enter the 16-digit credit card number.

Card Company: Please listen carefully as our menu has recently been changed. To report a stolen or lost card, press 1. To enquire about your account, press 2. To apply for a companion card, press 3. To hear about our latest promotion, press 4...

You: Press 2

Card Company: To listen to your recent transaction, press 1. To increase your credit limit, press 2. To dispute a recent transaction, press 3...

You: Press 0 (as you want to talk to a live agent!)

Card Company: Sorry, the number you have entered is not valid. Press # to hear your available selection again.

You: Press #. Press this and that and finally reach somebody after waiting for 5 minutes.

Card Company: Hello, thanks for calling ABC Card Company. We really appreciate your business. My name is John Smith. Can I get your credit card number again and confirm your residing address?

You: I thought I entered my credit card number already 10 minutes ago!?

Now, let us see what would happen when you call Diners Club:

Card Company: (within 3 rings) Hello, thanks for calling Diners Club. This is John Smith. How may I help you?

You: I want to...

Card Company: Good. May I get your Diners Club card number and your mailing address for confirmation?

You: My card number is......

Card Company: OK, here is what I can do for you regarding that recent questionable transaction…

See the difference? Yes, many banks have been able to drive down the operating costs by making aggressive use of advanced phone system and IVR systems. However, not all customers have time and patience to go through the system properly. To make it worse, some companies even disabled the "0" button because some callers simply press "0" hoping to reach a live operator. By changing the location of these keys regularly and hide the way to connect customers to their live agents, it only creates increasing usage frustration.

Having a good understanding of this support service problem, Diners Club card is able to use their superior customer service to retain customers. There are customers out there who appreciate and are willing to pay for the personalized customer service that is provided by Diners Club's bilingual call centre agents in Quebec. Furthermore, the monthly transaction history (i.e., the bill) that Diners Club mail you also summarize your transactions into different categories, such as food, transportation, hospitality, and so on. If you are using your credit card for business purpose, you know how cumbersome it is to prepare your monthly or quarterly report. By helping you to separate the transaction items, Diners Club is saving you time in these expense report preparation that to some people, is priceless!

How about Commodity Business?

Product differentiation is an interesting concept but can it be applied to commodity product or service? My students always want to know the answer because many of them are selling these inexpensive, basic products or services.

In my opinion, customers buy not just the core product or service in most cases. As I have shown you earlier in this book, people go to Starbucks not just for its coffee but also for its ambiance. When you go to your favorite hair salon every month or two, is it just for the hair cut, or is it also for the opportunity to talk to your hair stylist who may be acting as your good listener? See, people rarely focus only on the "core" product or service when spending money.

The first example that I can think of is the industry-use safety goggles that are used to protect workers from chemical hazards. These protective eyewears often come in ugly looking transparent frame that do not look fanciful. If you are a manufacturer of a safety goggle, should you simply drop the price to make it more competitive? Although it is feasible, other avenues can also be explored to differentiate your product such as focusing on the "physical difference" mentioned earlier in this chapter.

Sperian (previously known as Bacou-Dalloz) is a manufacturer of protective equipments. It manufactures several lines of protective eye wares that are highly distinctive from others. The company has incorporated the latest fashion in its goggle design and their product looks similar to designer sunglasses. Their goggles have wraparound frames that come in a wide range of colors and customers can choose different tints and colors for the lens. In addition, Sperian has introduced the Uvex Stealth® Reader Goggle with diopters ranging from +1.0 to +3.0, making it very suitable for those workers who need magnification for close-up inspection work.

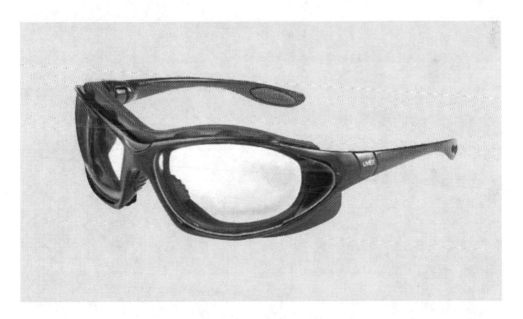

Sperian Protective Eyewear

Source: http://www.sperian.com/Supplementary/Documents_and_Downloads/Eye_and_Face_Protection/Eyewear/19062/1033.aspx

Perhaps you may say, "Yes, these cool-looking goggles are great but they must be very expensive. How can I justify such expensive purchase in my factory?" Well, let us think about the ROI from another perspective. Are your workers all wearing safety goggles? Do you have high employee turnover? What happens if your workers do not wear the safety goggles and were involved in accidents in your factory? Oh, a big increase of insurance premium and big trouble from your senior management! So, these fancy looking safety goggles may be your solution helping to save some money in the long run. When a pair of safety goggles look very good, I am sure the workers will be willing to wear them for work.

Let us consider another example —Paint. If you like doing home improvement projects, there is a good chance that you have had the experience of getting your hand dirty when opening the can of paint. Even pouring the paint out can be challenging to some people (including myself as I am not a professional!). To address these problems, a paint manufacturer called Dutch Boy is able to differentiate its products from its competitors, by creating a plastic paint container that has an easy-to-open lid. All you need is to twist the lid and pour out the paint by holding the handle on the container. No screwdriver or special tools are required.

Dutch Boy Paint

Is that not a wonderful design? No wonder people are willing to pay a price premium for the Dutch Boy paint. This is because people know it will cost them more as their hands will not get dirty as in the case with regular paints from other manufacturers.

How about the service industry? Well, there are many examples and it is all about walking the extra miles for your customers. Take the oil change service in the automotive industry, if you ask people why they go to "Mr. Lube" for changing oil, they will probably tell you that they enjoy the free newspaper, coffee and washing fluid top ups during their visit. Is it really free? No, if you look carefully on your Mr. Lube invoice you will find that the shop actually charges you a few dollars for these "extras". However, these coffee, newspaper and windshield fluids have successfully helped Mr. Lube to differentiate it from others. As seen from these examples, even simple products or services can be made special if you have a good understanding of customer needs and the challenges they face.

Chapter 9—Branding and Positioning

The 5-stage A.I.D.M.A. Framework

In the last few chapters, I have discussed the strategies to make your product or service unique to attract customers. But marketers and economists will both point out that customers are often irrational when making their purchasing decisions. People may buy your product or service simply because of your brand and its positioning in the market. To understand how branding and positioning are affecting customer satisfaction, I suggest we look at the A.I.D.M.A. framework to put things into context. Basically this framework outlines the 5 stages that eventually lead to the completion of a successful transaction. The stages are:

Awareness

The first step is to make use of advertising, word-of-mouth promotion, or publicity to generate awareness of your brand among your target customer segments

Interest

Subsequently, you have to make sure your brand positioning and/or USPs (i.e. features) are interesting to your customer segments. Otherwise, these prospective customers will not spend the time to learn more about your detailed product or service offerings in detail.

Desire

Getting prospective customers excited about your brand or offering is not sufficient. You have to create a trigger point (e.g. an opportunity) to make them have such a strong desire to purchase your product or service. Perhaps a time-limited special promotion can be launched, or create scarcity of your goods. For example, people are lining up in front of Apple stores around the world to get their iPad or iPhone because they have a strong desire to acquire these latest high-tech gadgets.

Memory

Everyday, people come across thousands of brand names in their daily lives. The fact is that people skim through advertisements quickly and they do not spend too much time memorizing the name of the advertisers. You have seen the battery-powered drum-playing pink bunny on TV commercial but do you remember which brand of alkaline battery it is? Is it Duracell or Energizer? From your weekly flyers, you know your nearby department store is running a no-tax sales event this coming Saturday. However, are you sure it is Sears and not the Bay? How about the phone number for ordering that "As Seen On TV" product? Is it 1-800-123-4567 or 1-877-123-4567? As you can see, not all customers can correctly name your product or service; therefore you have to find ways to ensure they come to you and not your competitors. Branding helps to reinforce your product or service in people's mindset.

Action

The last step is to ensure your prospective customers make the purchase successfully. Do you have sufficient stocks of your products at the retail level? How about the sales people who work at the retailer? Do you give them any incentives to promote your brand versus others? If you are selling products online, can your web server handle the increased traffic load during a sales event and not crashing it? How about the call centre reps who greet people on the phone? Are they well aware of your product, service and the special promotion that you are running? If your prospect cannot buy your products (e.g. out-of-stock) or use your service (e.g. no available appointment), they may not give you a second chance to get their business. By understanding the AIDMA framework, it become obvious that branding and product/service positioning are important in any sales cycle.

What is a brand and why is it important?

To help my students to understand branding, I have tried to explain it visually by creating something called the Branding Wheel:

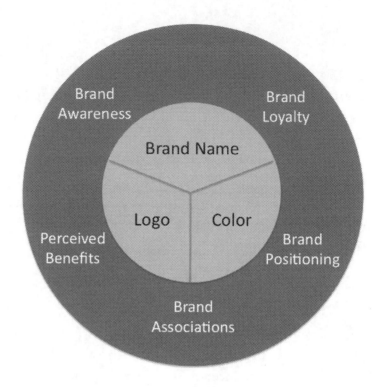

The Branding Wheel

As you can see from this diagram, a brand is made up of core elements such as brand name, logo, and color. With this information, you can visually present a brand to your audience. For example, "twitter" is the brand name, its logo is represented by the bird in light blue color.

However, the brand elements do not stop here. In my opinion, the description of a brand is not complete unless the following five aspects of brand equity are included. They are:

- **Brand Awareness**   (e.g. How many people can recognize your brand and also name your product/service correctly?)

- **Brand Loyalty** (e.g. What percentage of your customers are repeated ones?)

- **Brand Associations** (e.g. Bridgehead = Organic Coffee; Lululemon = Yoga)

- **Brand Positioning** (e.g. The Law of Leadership —It is better to be first than to be better: Viagra pills)

- **Perceived Benefits of the Brand** (e.g. Cisco = industry standard = low business risk)

Marketers should care about branding because it helps to improve their company's profitability. Let me give you an example to illustrate this point. Unlike other countries, Canada's tap water is drinkable. In fact, the water processing plants and distribution system in each city is highly regulated and the water quality has to be tested many times to ensure that it is up to government standard. According to the City of Toronto, the 2010 rate for tap water at home is $2.0616 per m³ but a 591ml bottle of Dasani water is being sold at about $2 at the retail level. As you can see, public tap water is very inexpensive in Canada! What most consumers do not know is that the Dasani bottled water is actually coming from your local municipal water distribution system. That's right, Dasani water is actually tap water. So, how can Coca Cola Company justify the selling of tap water at such a high price? It is all about branding. Dasani has been aggressively promoting its "filtered 5 times" product positioning to make people think that their bottled water is much better than others. This clearly illustrates how branding and positioning can be used to extract value from consumers!

3 Functions of a Brand

In my opinion, a brand serves three major functions and you should pay attention to these when developing or revising your brand. The functions are:

Recognition

Brands help to simply customer's search process. Imagine what would happen if all soft drinks are being sold in plain white-color tin cans. That would be a nightmere because you have to spend time to locate your favorite product. With proper branding, you know the red color cans with a white and red swirl are Coca Cola and the green color cans with a red dot in the middle are 7-Up!

Risk Reduction

If you are travelling to a foreign country and need a quick meal, the Golden Arch at McDonald's may make you smile. That's because you know the food at McDonald's are safe to eat, relatively inexpensive, and they serve the food quickly. Taste aside, you know you cannot go wrong by dining at McDonald's for a quick meal. Brands offer a certain guarantee of product quality and service levels.

Identification

People use brands to radiate their identity to others. As my friend Brian is a tennis player and he will tell you that wearing a Lacoste Golf shirt is "making a statement". Similarly, there are people who like to show off their association with certain brand as it fits with their lifestyle or attitude. Harley-Davidson motorcycles come to my mind as an example.

Brand Positioning

As mentioned just now, brand positioning is an important aspect of brand equity. It simply means finding a position in the mindset of the consumer in relation to the competition. If Canadians are asked what they think about the Hyundai cars back in early 1980s, they would tell you that the Hyundai brand represents "cheap Korean car". It is not surprising because the quality of the car at that time was not superior as compared to the Japanese and American ones.

However, Hyundai has aggressively improved its product quality throughout the years and it has hired top-tier advertising agencies to look after its brand image and positioning. In recent years, Hyundai has moved up its positioning as their Genesis, Elantra and Sonata cars have been continuously earning great awards and recognitions from Automobile Journalists Association of Canada (AJAC) and J.D. Power and Associates. Today, the same question about the Hyundai brand will elicit a very different answer from those in the 1980s when Hyundai first entered the Canadian auto market.

Positioning (Perceptual) Map

To explore brand positioning, companies often make use of something called a positioning map. It is also known as a perceptual map. Basically, you draw two axes with key product attributes (e.g. Price and Quality) and then put your brand together with your major competitors on the map. With this positioning mapping exercise, you can:

1. Find out how your brand is being perceived by internal and external customers
2. Identify any product or service gaps
3. Find out your weaknesses
4. Develop or fine-tune your unique selling propositions
5. Identify area for growth
6. Identify brand or product for removal

An example of positioning map is shown below:

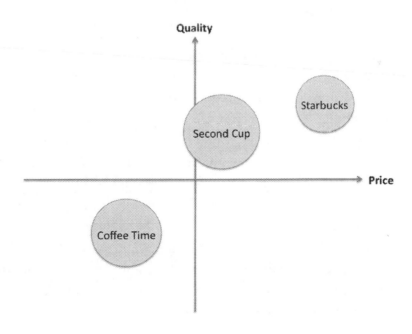

Positioning Map for Coffee Shops

Chapter 10—Retaining Your Customers

Why Spend Time on Customer Retention?

The last chapter of this book talks about one of the most important aspects of CRM —customer retention. Similar to many marketers including myself, I spent most of my time designing great products and planning exciting advertising campaigns when I was working in the telecommunication industry years ago. The concept of customer retention is kind of vague and all I have heard all day in the industry was "Oh! It's 5 or 6 times more expensive to attract a new customer than retaining an existing one."

The field of customer retention only caught my attention when I was attending a CEO Summit that was organized by a venture capitalist in the early 2000s. It was the speech of a start-up CEO who made a statement that goes like this: "Our company has spent X amount of dollars in carrying out so and so exciting advertising campaigns. We utilized penetration pricing strategy and successfully acquired Y amount of new telecom subscribers last year, which beat our original estimates." Sounds alright so far, I thought. However, the bigger problematic picture emerged immediately during the second part of his speech — "Although we have got a great year in new customer acquisition, our EBITDA remained severely negative due to high customer churn levels." At that moment, one of the VCs sitting up on the stage asked the start-up CEO about the churn rate. The reply was shocking to me and also to the audience. The start-up CEO replied embarrassingly "We suffered a 100% churn rate last year." In other words, this company lost all of its original customers acquired two years ago; therefore, although it acquired many new customers last year, it does not help the company too much on the financial side. A 100% churn rate is somewhat unreal but true.

It is only after that CEO summit that I started to think really hard about the importance of customer retention. I have put together my thoughts on some of the customer retention strategies in this chapter and I hope you will find them useful.

The Concept of A.R.A.

I guess a fundamental concept that marketers need to know is the A.R.A. one. Marketers should really design marketing activities based on these three important aspects. A.R.A stands for Customer Acquisition, Customer Retention, and Add-on Selling to your existing customers. I think each of them is equally important to the survivability of an organization. In my opinion, focusing on these activities will help maximize sales revenue and profits.

Acquisition of Customer

The first step is to draw prospective customers into your doors and convert them into customers. As can be learned from all marketing textbooks, advertising, sales promotion, and public relations can be utilized to make it happen; therefore I am not going to discuss these in details here. One thing that must be remembered is that the right kind of customers should be acquired; tricking them to use your product or service is not good. Customers who realize they are tricked may spend their money with you once only and then leave forever. In some extreme cases, getting the wrong customers is the beginning of bad publicity. It only takes seconds for people to post nasty comments about your product or service on their social networking pages!

Last month, my parents and I went to a new Malaysian restaurant for dinner because of its print advertisement in the local newspaper. According to the print advertisement, this recently opened restaurant offered dinner buffet with hundreds of authentic Malaysian dishes priced at $28 per person with senior citizen's discounts available. Yes, this restaurant received our money that night but we decided not to give it any business in the future. Why? Firstly, the dishes were not that authentic and the taste was pale. Then, this so-called buffet had about 10 to 15 dishes on the table, not the hundreds that it claimed on the advertisement. What angered my parents was the lack of senior citizen's discounts that were promised. The manager said, "Oh, senior discounts only apply to regular menu and not the buffet one!" Then, it added 15% service charges automatically on the bill, which is an abnormal business practice in my city.

As my parents are opinion leaders in their circle of friends, you can guess how much publicity damage the restaurant suffered as a result of our visit. As you have learned from this book, there are different kinds of consumers, so perhaps the restaurant should target another group of customers. There is an old saying, "You can trick your customer once, but not twice."

Retention of Customer

When your industry or business is in an infant stage, it is growing so fast that you are spending all of your energy fulfilling new orders from customers and do not have much time to think about customer retention. However, you should always remember that growth does not last forever no matter how great it is.

If your market is an attractive one, new market entrants will join the game to steal your market share. Eventually, the growth will slow down as the market matures. Leaving customer retention strategies till the last minute may be too late because by then your customer base could be shrinking. This is because most consumers will make their churn decision prior to the end of their contract terms in the service industry, or they are just waiting for a special price promotion of a competitor's product before leaving your brand. Later in this chapter, I am going to discuss some good customer retention strategies but in general, the formula of: "Higher customer satisfaction = Higher retention rate" always hold true.

Add-on Selling

Marketers often ignore the importance of up-selling to their existing customers. Take ING Direct, the direct banking service provided by ING as example. When ING Direct entered the Canadian market back in 1997, it only had one major product —Investment Savings Account in Canadian dollars. Subsequently, the bank gradually added other products one-by-one including US$ Investment Savings Account, RSP Investment Savings Account, and eventually in 2010 the Tax-Free Savings Account. The bank also launched business service in recent years.

So, instead of just chasing new customers to switch from the five major Canadian banks, how about launching some CRM initiatives to up sell these new banking services to existing customers? Remember, not all customers are interested in following your company's development once they have started using your service or product. For ING Direct, I will not be surprised if some of their existing customers, especially those who joined them in the late 90s, still believe that ING Direct has only one type of saving account as of today.

If you have time, try to do the following small exercise, you may be shocked to see the results:

1. List the number of products/services that you have launched in the past 10 years

2. Randomly contact some of your existing customers to see if they can name all of these products

3. Find out when was the last time your organization up sold these customers

According to my students, the common answers to these questions are:

1. Tons, too many to list on a sheet of paper
2. 80% of customers do not know about the new products that were launched in the past decade
3. Upsell to existing customers? We do not do that. We only try to sell additional services to those who have just signed up

I hope your organization is doing a much better job in Add-on Selling than my students!

Importance of Customer Life-Time Value (CLV)

Have you ever wondered why your wireless service provider such as Rogers, Bell and Telus are promoting their "$0" phone? Are their phone really that cheap? The fact is that wireless carriers have to buy their phones from the manufacturer:

- Regular GSM/CDMA cellphone costs $100 to $200 per unit
- Smartphone costs $500 or more per unit

As there is no free lunch, you are actually paying for the phone implicitly over the term of your contract. Market research has consistently reported that the acquisition cost for Canadian mobile service provider is about $390. This amount includes handset subsidies, marketing promotions, and certain sales administration costs. A wireless provider is going to lose money if a $25/month plan customer goes away in just one year. Hence, using these $0 phone or heavy handset subsidies are good tactics to "lock" customers into a multi-year service contract. That is also why a heavy early cancellation fee (ECF) of up to $200 has to be paid to the wireless carrier if you want to break a contract to churn away.

Another tactic that telecommunication companies use is "bundling". Let us say you are using wireless, cable TV and also cable Internet from Rogers; you probably will not bother to churn away when a new wireless entrant offers you deep discount. This is because eliminating one service means the loss (or reduction) of bundled discount and that having an extra invoice is another hassle to worry about per month. If you are currently using each service from separate providers, perhaps it is the right time to consolidate your services to a single provider!

The above discussions lead us to consider the concept of customer life-time value as it considers not just the short-term monthly revenue and profitability that is contributed by the customer, but their overall financial contribution during their tenure with the company. If Customer A spends $30 per month with you and Customer B spends only $20, you may accidentally think that Customer A is more valuable. It "can" be true, but you need another piece of information, that is, how long will these customers stay with you. Customer A will not be a great customer if he or she only stays with you for just a few months, while Customer B may have been a very loyal customer who has been using your product or service for years. In this case, customer B is definitely more valuable to your organization from the customer life-time value perspective.

How to Calculate CLV?

Before I explain how CLV can be calculated, a few words about terminology. Customer Life-Time Value (CLV) has another name. It is also known as Life-time Market Value (LMV). CLV can be calculated at individual customer or segment levels. If you see the word "Customer Equity", then it means the summation of CLV among all customer segments of interest.

The basic methodology to calculate CLV is to take customer's average transaction amount and multiply it by the number of transactions conducted over time. For example, if your customer on average buys $500 worth of product every quarter and stays for roughly 2.5 years, then your customer's CLV is:

$500 x 4 x 2.5 = $5000

That is, each customer is worth $5000 to your organization. Your goal is to increase this CLV number by getting customer to stay longer and consuming more of your product or services during their association with your organization. What I have just shown you is a very basic approach to CLV to help understand the concept. In reality, the calculation can be more complicated when you are using profitability (rather than revenue) and also incorporating net present value (ie., discount rate) in the calculation.

Students often ask me if they should use revenue or profit in their calculation. My opinion on this is that it really depends on availability of data. Answer these questions:

1. Do you know about the average customer acquisition cost?
2. Do you know about the cost of goods sold?
3. Do you know the discount rate (for Net Present Value (NPV) calculation) that is used by the organization?
4. Do you know about the retention rate?
5. Do you know about retention-related costs?

If your answers to these questions are "Yes", then proceed to use profitability. Otherwise, it is equally satisfactory to use revenue as a proxy to profitability assuming that you can clearly state this upfront in your CLV calculation.

What is Churn?

Customer relationship is one of the most valuable assets of an organization. However, it is also one of the most undervalued assets of an organization. As the source of all your revenues and profits, customers should be valued and their relationships with you should be protected.

In our discussion of CRM, you will often hear about the term "Churn". Other names with the same meaning includes:

- Customer Churn
- Customer Defection
- Loss of Customer Relationship

Basically, churn is the "go away" action and churned customers are those who have left your business. A related term called "Customer Attrition" is often used. Unlike churn, attrition describes a situation in which a customer is reducing the amount of transaction with your organization even as continuing to be an active or paying customer technically speaking. To illustrate their difference, let me use a real-life example in the banking industry. Let us say you are using TD Canada Trust and have five accounts with them (saving, checking, GIC, credit card and mortgage). If you move all of these five accounts to CIBC, then you have "churned" from TD Canada Trust and no longer become their customers. However, if you only move the key accounts such as checking, GIC, credit card, and mortgage to CIBC but leave the savings account there with TD Canada Trust, it is attrition and not churn because you are still considered to be a TD customer.

When to Address Churn?

That is a multi-million dollar question because people know that churn should be addressed early on in theory but practically speaking, the issue of churn often does not get addressed by the organization until customers have expressed their intentions to go away.

Many credit card companies and telecommunications providers set up separate teams to handle account-closing matters. To reduce churn, customers are often provided with deep discounts (e.g., lower interest rate on the credit card or special wireless rate plan) in the hope that customers will change their mind after talking to these super-nice people over the phone. That is why whenever you mention about the "intention" to churn, your call will be escalated to this churn department because the level-one agents on the phone are not authorized to offer you these special offers. After listening to this point, some of my students were able to save money by calling up their service provider. I am not asking you to pretend churning as it is unethical, but I think it is always a good idea to discuss your changing banking/telecom needs with your service provider occasionally. Maybe they will be able to offer you some special deals that are not advertised on their web site to retain you as a happy customer.

Marketers know that trying to isolate customer churn and address it as a separate issue is a misguided approach. It is often too late to address churn when customers are in the process of leaving and it can be very expensive to retain them once they have left your organization. In my opinion, companies should not wait until customers are about to leave before taking action to control churn. If your organization considers churn management as a strategic move, its management should make efforts to focus on loyalty and retention initiatives at all stages of the customer lifecycle. The ultimate objective is to properly manage the quality of the entire user experience from day one.

Customer retention is about making sure existing customers keep buying from you. I know it is easy to say, but difficult to do. Ask this question, "When did you discuss customer retention in your meeting with management?" Last week, last month, or last year? Very often, I hear people saying "Oh, I'm not working in the customer care department so it's not my business to discuss this topic!" without knowing that customer retention requires the support of employees of all ranks and departments, from front line sales people all the way to back-end support staffs.

Dr. Ken K. Wong

Why are Customers Leaving?

Many of my students believe that the main reasons why people churn away from a brand is because of its inferior product or service. Well, they have made a good guess but it is not necessarily true. Prior research has shown that there are all kinds of reasons why customers churn away from their existing service provider or merchant. In descending order, these reasons include:

1. No Customer Contact Strategy

About 67% of consumers left an organization because they feel that the company does not care about their existence. That is why insurance companies keep sending you a birthday card every year and your service provider may give you some "perks" or gifts occasionally to appreciate your business.

2. Product Dissatisfaction

About 15% of consumers churned away because they are not happy with your product or service. Perhaps it is a design flaw in the first place, or maybe the product features are outdated and no longer become relevant to the user. So, the question is what do you do when customers are not happy? Have you established the right channel to let them vent out their dissatisfaction and provide remedies? Or, do you just ignore these dissatisfied customers and let them bad-mouth your organization? Apple's iPhone 4 has reception problems but at least the company is willing to admit their design fault and offer customers a free plastic case to fix the problem temporarily.

3. Competition

Basically, this means that your competitor has been making more offerings than yours and 9% of your churned customers agree with this point of view. Although there may be no problem with your product or service, your competitors may be running special sales promotions or deep discounts to get your customers' businesses.

4. Friendship in the other company.

Some people go to a particular pub for drinks not because of the beer (as all pubs sell a similar selection of beer) but because of their friendship with the hostess or manager. In the insurance industry, you may be moving your insurance coverage from one firm to another not because of their better rate, but because your best friend just got a new job there as an insurance agent.

About 5% of people churn away simply because they can get better friendship or relationship with the other company.

5. Relocation or Death

If you have stayed in Canada for the past 20 years, you know people like to move around. Some people move from smaller towns to bigger cities, whereas others such as my friends move back to their home country in Asia and Europe for good. You lost these customers simply because they are not residing in your serving area anymore. Of course, some people just cannot come to your shop any longer as they have passed away. About 4% of people churned away due to relocation or death.

Cannibalization

In the discussion of customer churn, the problem of cannibalization is something that companies should not overlook. So, what exactly is cannibalization? Well, when your customer moves from using a high-end service to a low-end one, then you are suffering from the problem of cannibalization although the customer has not technically churned away from your organization. Cannibalization occurs often when your company has introduced a newer and less expensive service that can fit with customers' need better, than using the existing more expensive one.

I still remember a decade or so ago when Air Canada launched its discounted airline called Tango. Before Tango's launch, I flew from Toronto to Calgary often using Air Canada. As my business meetings in Calgary are mostly on a last minute notice, my executive assistant had to book my seat on full fare at over $1600. Yes, I know it will only cost me a few hundred dollars if I made advanced reservations but that is another story.

Then, the Tango flights were introduced with the same airport, same type of aircrafts, and even the same terminal. The only difference is the lack of full-service meals on the Tango flight. But as I usually take the early flights, there was no need to eat a lot on the plane. So, I was able to significantly reduce my flight expense from $1600 to just two or three hundred dollars. As Tango is owned by Air Canada, I am still technically considered to be an Air Canada customer but the revenue contribution has been reduced greatly. That is cannibalization.

To avoid such mistakes, it would have been better if Air Canada could make the Tango flight very different in the first place to target value travelers. When your low-end product is so good and appealing, it is going to attract your high-end customers to give it a try, which can be dangerous financially.

Fourteen Ways to Retain Your Customer

You have read on why customer retention is key to the success of an organization. So, how to do it? In theory, if your company can effectively segment your customers into groups and target them with the right product/service offerings, it is more likely that the customer will respond favorably in the longer run causing an increase in retention rate.

I have worked in industries ranging from small start-ups to multinational ones. I pay close attention to their customer retention strategies and surprisingly keeping customers happy and loyal does not require too much special efforts. Perhaps a slight change in the way you conduct business is all you need. In the following pages, I am going to summarize the 14 different ways to retain your customers.

1. Get a knowledgeable person to handle the phone call

Remember the Diners Club example that I gave earlier? Consumers these days are far more knowledgeable (thanks to the Internet) so I guess most people will not call you if they are able to find the information on the Internet. Hence, try to avoid having too many layers of staffs (e.g. Level 1, Level 2, Level 3…etc) to handle incoming phone calls. It can be very frustrating to waste time talking to the Level 1 staffs on the phone who escalates the calls to another team 95% of the time. In other words, you have to do a reality check to see what kind of values these front line people are bringing to you and your customers. Have you recently checked the kind of questions your customers are raising?

2. Explain to your employees about the importance of customer retention

Believe it or not, some employees who work in large companies may not care too much about customer retention as they may think, "Well, we have got thousands if not millions of customers. It won't hurt to lose a few troublesome ones." That kind of thought should not be adopted. Yes, you may have numerous customers today but what if I'm telling you that you are losing a few consistently over time? In the computing industry during the 1980s and 1990s, you rarely saw Microsoft spend any marketing dollars to ask people not to switch to Macs because the Wintel platform (Windows + Intel) had over 90% of the market share. However, since 2008, Microsoft has been spending money on TV (remember its "I'm a PC" TV commercial?) and the Internet (see the "PC vs Mac" pages on the Windows 7 site) to tell people it is not a good idea to switch to Mac. I guess my point is that you must make sure all employees understand that customer retention is key to an organization's success, because the great hey days will not last forever no matter which industry you are operating in.

3. Get all of your employees to work together to keep your existing customers satisfied

Have you ever visited the Doubletree Hotel? If you are not happy with your stay, just tell any of their staff members (including the janitor or the room service staffs) and your stay will be free. In other hotel chains, perhaps the hotel manager is the only person who can waive your bill, but at the Doubletree hotel, all of the employees were empowered to do things right to keep customers happy. Of course, the hotel has set up a tracking system to look for abusers of this policy. In other words, everybody plays a role in customer retention in your organization.

4. Increase cross-sell ratio

That is my any way of saying "let's use more bundling". As in the Rogers TV/Cable/Internet example given earlier, by having your customer use more than one product or service, it helps to reduce their price sensitivity and better defend yours against the competitive offerings. Well, if your competitor is a large one that can also put together a similar bundle, then you have to go back to the drawing board to think about something more creative to achieve better product differentiation.

5. Increase barriers to switch

Try to set up high switching barriers in your product or service. Have you ever wondered why those laptop power adapters all look different among various brands? That is because it is a switching barrier that is created artificially by those laptop manufacturers. For example, my Fujitsu P2040 laptop power charger can be used in the P7120 model that I have purchased subsequently. I have also invested some money on an Electrovaya PowerPad external battery for this Fujitsu model. Now, let us say I need to replace my Fujitsu P7120 laptop with a newer one, do you think I will get an IBM or Fujitsu one when the laptop specifications are similar?

If you have driven a Honda Accord sedan before, you know it has an orange-color oil change indicator that pops up to remind you for regular maintenance service every X kilometers. This indicator will remain on until you take the car to an authorized Honda dealer for service. This is a great switching barrier because most Mr. Lube or Midas technicians will not have the right tool (or know-how) to turn this indicator off even after an oil change. My wife pesters me to go back to Honda for oil change because this lid-up indicator bothers her if I do the servicing elsewhere.

Switching barriers can also come in the form of termination penalty, loss of bundle discounts, or simply educating customers about the high activation or installation cost with the new vendor. Some customers change their suppliers to get better deals without noticing that any change involves "risks". Is the new product made by ISO9001 standard? Is it compatible with your existing process? Will your insurance premium go up? Will your staff know how to operate the new machine without incurring injuries? See, there are many things that you can talk about to help your customers make an educated decision about churning.

6. Target your customers with the right offer.

As you have learned from your marketing textbook, some consumers are early adopters, whereas others may be laggards. With a wider range of services available, companies should understand their customers' needs better and develop greater insight into their purchasing behaviors. Engage your early adopters in your product testing cycle (e.g. allow them to be your beta testers) and perhaps create scarcity to create excitement. On the other hand, if your customers are mostly laggards, then avoid talking too much about the hypes as all they need may be a good, reliable, and affordable product that addresses their "needs" rather than "wants".

7. Customer relationships need to be continuously evolved through ongoing testing and refinement of bundles, messages, and incentives

From the earlier section in this chapter, you have learned that the most important reason why customers churn away is because they feel that the company does not care about their existence. So, try to contact your customers more often. Not just at the time of purchase or activation. How about making it a company policy to follow up with your customers 1 or 2 weeks after the purchase? Canadian Tires has been great in this area. About 2 weeks after serving your car at a Canadian Tires store, you will get a phone call from them asking if things are satisfactory and they may ask you to do a quick survey to understand your satisfaction level. This is a great move because the company will be able to identify those unhappy customers and address any outstanding issues if required.

Keep talking to your customers from time to time, and establish the right channel for communication. In the old days, it was all about the physical "Comment Box". Today, it's all about social networking platforms like Facebook and Twitter.

8. Promote customer testimonials regularly

Do you know that your competitors are spreading negative words about you, your department, your product, and your company everyday to your prospective and existing customers? You need to spread some positive words out there to counteract their actions. This can be done through regular promotion of customer testimonials in your newsletter and/or company web site. If there are industry-recognized customer satisfaction surveys or awards being instituted, try to get your company to participate. The Korean car company, Hyundai, has been able to win many of those J.D. Associates awards in the last decade. By promoting these awards in their advertisements, Hyundai was able to create a positive product positioning in customers' mindset and defend any bad perceptions about Korean cars.

If there are unhappy customers out there who are making noise on the net, try to find them and rectify the situation swiftly. You have to deliver the message that any unsatisfactory user experience is an isolated case and not a general feeling among all customers.

9. Be proactive in informing your customers about future problem

If you are in the service industry especially in the high technology sector, you know there will be times that your online service will be interrupted, such as during the regular maintenance windows that will result in network outage. If you are an airliner and you plan to cancel some flights because of low seat bookings, try to alert those affected passengers who have booked the flight earlier. If possible, walk the extra mile to help them reduce the impact of such flight changes.

If you are the manufacturer of goods, you need to introduce new products and withdraw older models from time to time. If you want plan to discontinue the manufacturing or support of certain products, try to alert your customers in advanced so that they can plan ahead about such changes.

10. Manage corporate changes properly

You know anybody can say anything about your organization out there in the market. Rumors are unavoidable; this is especially true whenever there is any takeover, merger, acquisition or bankruptcy. To ensure your existing customers understand that you are still in business during these corporate changes, try to retain your existing phone numbers (for sales and tech support), web site address, and mailing address as much as possible. Even if you have to change them as a result of the mergers and acquisitions (M&A) activity, allow the change to gradually take place over certain period of time, with proper notification to your existing customers. When your customers cannot find you on the web using the existing web site address or are getting a "the line has been disconnected" voice message when calling your office, they may think that you are out-of-business already and will begin to shop for a new vendor.

11. Handle service termination request carefully and intelligently

Let your win-back team to handle the request, not your regular Level 1 call center agents. Equip your win-back team with all of the tools/empowerment required to take action to cheer up your soon-to-be-gone customers. Experience has told us that you need to staff your win-back team with people who are very nice, very patient and are good listeners. If possible, locate your win-back team locally.

12. Manage win-back strategies properly

The first thing that you should know is that dropping the price of your product or service does not guarantee successful retention. Before you drop the price, acknowledge customers' concerns and try to identify the root of the problem. Try to solve the problem for the customers. Is the customer looking for a customized solution? Is the customer getting upset because he or she was getting impolite treatment from certain staff members? Very often, there is nothing wrong with the product or service itself; so it is best for you to see where the expectation gap is located and correct it.

Practically speaking, some small actions may cheer up a customer; this includes: getting an acknowledgement letter from the company's senior management, a personal voice mail from the CEO office, or perhaps just a small company-branded gift will do the trick. Even if you are unable to solve the customers' problem, acknowledging that the problem exists may be the best next step to retain your customer.

13. Business Continuity Plan

In Canada, it is not uncommon to see companies facing threats or labor disputes from the union. If you have lived in Canada long enough, you know all sectors can be affected by the actions of strike or work-to-rule. As a manager, you need to plan ahead and develop your business continuity plan before these events happen. There are several tactics that you can use. From the human resource's perspective, you can:

1. Get non-union members to do job shadowing
2. Get staffs from another office (e.g. in another province) to do job shadowing
3. Train managers to perform front line duties (e.g. sales and basic technical support)
4. Explore the costs and process to secure third party or contractors to the job

Another typical issue that affects business continuity is information technology (IT)-related. Remember the massive power outage in mid-2000s? How about the severe flooding that have occurred in some parts of British Columbia, Alberta, and Quebec? To ensure your computer servers are safe and running all the time, remember the need to build system "redundancy" and do not put all eggs in one basket. For example, Canadian banks always build redundant data centres across the country to ensure their computer systems will still be up and running in case disastrous incident happens in a particular building or geographical area. "We've got a strike" or "There's a flood in the building" is no longer a good excuse for service interruption these days. To keep your customers happy, plan ahead!

14. Customers who switched may come back

Yes, your customers might have churned away already several weeks ago despite utilizing all 13 tactics that I have presented here. However, do not forget that your churned customers might not be totally satisfied with your competitor.

If you happen to have the opportunity to get in touch with your churned customer again, try to learn if they are happy with the new providers. Perhaps after 2 or 3 months of switching, your customers may want to give you a second chance and come back to you. There is an interesting saying, "when both options are not ideal, people would choose the less evil one". Perhaps the new provider's service level or product quality is worse than yours!

Having said that, there are certain rules and regulations that govern how companies can offer win-back specials. This is especially true in the telecommunication industry; investigate these restrictions first, if any.

Epilogue

I hope you have enjoyed reading this book and found it interesting.

Frankly speaking, CRM is difficult to teach because it is easy to say but very difficult to implement. Senior management often ignores the fact that customers' needs and wants are evolving everyday, hence giving managers little support in their CRM initiatives. Unfortunately, I cannot really teach you how to "wake up your boss" and get them out of their "comfort zone". As I have mentioned earlier in my book, successful CRM requires support from staff members at all levels and sometimes a "top-down" approach is required to ensure successful implementation.

In this book, I have presented several methods to segment your customers, ways to retain them, and also strategies to make your product or service unique. I hope you have found this information useful and enlightening. CRM is a broad field that covers many topics. In addition to reading books, you are also suggested to attend those industry seminars or trade shows to learn about the latest developments. Leading CRM solution providers such as Microsoft, IBM, Oracle and Salesforce.com often hold these events with their business partners across the country, so check them out when you get a chance.

To those who are browsing this book right now at Chapters/Indigo, just pay for it and evaluate the book leisurely at home for 2 weeks. Don't stand in the aisle for the whole afternoon! Remember to keep your original receipt if you intend to get a full refund at the bookstore later.

If you have purchased this book as part of Dr. Wong's course, thank you. Do not forget to buy me a cup of coffee or drop me an e-mail if you get a job promotion later. However, if you have just downloaded this book from those illegal web sites and would like to keep it on your computer for future reference, you have three options:

1. Go to iUniverse's official web site to purchase a legitimate electronic copy. I have intentionally made the ebook version affordable (about US$10) so that my students can enjoy it without costing them an arm and a leg. Helping you understand the concept of intellectual properties is part of my teaching objectives.

2. Make a donation to your local charity or become a volunteer. I really mean it. If you absolutely do not want to pay the publisher for whatever reasons, please at least make a difference to help other people in your community.

3. Do nothing, if you think stealing is the right thing to do.

Have a great day and thanks for taking time to read my work.

Cheers,

Ken

References

Arens, W. F., Weigold, M. F., & Arens, C. (2008). *Contemporary Advertising* (12th ed.). New York: McGraw Hill Higher Education.

Armstrong, G., & Kotler, P. (2009). *Principles of Marketing* (13th ed.). Alexandria, VA: Prentice Hall.

Belch, G. E., & Belch, M. A. (2008). *Advertising and Promotion: An Integrated Marketing Communications Perspective* (8th ed.). New York: McGraw-Hill/Irwin.

Boyd, H., Mullins, J., & Walker, O. (2009). *Marketing Management: A Strategic Decision-making Approach* (7th ed.). New York: McGraw-Hill.

Cannon, J., Jr.., McCarthy, E. J., & Perreault, W. (2008). *Basic Marketing* (17th ed.). New York: McGraw-Hill/Irwin.

Cateora, P. R., & Graham, J. (2006). *International Marketing* (13th ed.). New York: McGraw-Hill/Irwin.

Cateora, P. R., Graham, J. L., & Papadopoulos, N. (2008). *International Marketing* (2nd Canadian ed.) Toronto: McGraw-Hill Ryerson.

Crane, F. G., Kerin, R. A., Hartley, S. W., Berkowitz, E. N. & Rudelius, W. (2006). *Marketing*. (6th Canadian ed.). Toronto: McGraw-Hill Ryerson

Dalgic, T. & Leeuw, M. (1993). "Niche Marketing Revisited: Theoretical and Practical Issues," in Michael Levy and Dhruv Grewal (eds.), *Academy of Marketing Science Proceedings*, Miami Beach, May 26-29, 1993, pp. 137-145.

Dalgic, T. & Leeuw, M. (1994). "Niche Marketing Revisited: Concept, Applications and Some European Cases," *European Journal of Marketing*, 28 (4), pp 39-55.

Hill, C. W. (2010). *International Business* (8th ed.). New York: McGraw Hill Higher Education.

Kotler, P. & Keller, K. L. (2008). *Marketing Management* (13th ed.). Alexandria, VA: Prentice Hall.

Porter, M.E. (1979, March/April). How Competitive Forces Shape Strategy, *Harvard Business Review*, 57 (2), pp. 137-145.

Porter, M.E. (2008, January). The Five Competitive Forces That Shape Strategy, Special Issue on HBS Centennial, *Harvard Business Review*, 86 (1).

Reynolds, T.J and Olson, J.C (eds.) (2001). *Understanding Consumer Decision Making: The Means-End Approach to Marketing and Advertising Strategy*. Lawrence Erlbaum Associates Mahwah, New Jersey, USA.

Index

95